The
Macmillan
Short
Course
Programme

Level 2

Matthew Farthing &
Alan Pulverness

CONTENTS

TOPIC	UNIT 1 – pages 2-17 Looking Around	UNIT 2 – pages 18-33 What's On?
LANGUAGE STUDY	Tense review - past tenses - time words - listing events in the past	Active/passive voice
LANGUAGE PRACTICE	Asking questions Writing grammar notes	Passive voice - impersonal passives - modals
SKILLS	Agreeing/disagreeing (S) Discussing certainty/uncertainty (S) Travelling to Britain (W) Describing the British (W) Describing places (R)	Discussing sport (S) Describing a game (S) Recognising polite/impolite registers (L) Descriptions of pubs (R) Leisure activities (R)
VOCABULARY BUILDING SKILLS	Storing and organising new words Word sets	Dictionary skills
LEXICAL AREAS	Weather	Sport
PROJECTS	A town portrait	Entertainments guide
LEARNER TRAINING	Thinking about language learning Course Diary	Reading and listening to English in Britain Course Diary

Note: In the skills section, S = Speaking, L = Listening, W = Writing, R = Reading

UNIT 3 – pages 34-49 Music and Youth Culture	UNIT 4 – pages 50-65 Storytelling	TOPIC
Conditional sentences	Linking words - contrasts - reasons and results - purpose Relative clauses	LANGUAGE STUDY
Conditional sentences Talking about possibility	Expressing purpose Stating results	LANGUAGE PRACTICE
Discussing music (S/L) Analysing opinions (L) Reading a poem (R) Rock music (R/W) Dialogue writing (W)	Telling a story (S) Listening to a story (L) Short story (R) Early memories (W)	SKILLS
Word association	Focus on emotive language	VOCABULARY BUILDING SKILLS
Music	Family relationships	LEXICAL AREAS
Youth market survey	Personal project - class magazine - storytelling - drama - recorded interviews - video - school prospectus - game - special study	PROJECTS
Project evaluation Thinking about language learning Course Diary	Analysing learning Planning future learning Course Diary	LEARNER TRAINING

LOOKING AROUND • SECTION 1

❶ Look carefully at the photographs below. What are the things you can see? What do you know about them? Where do you think you might see them?

❷ How many of the things in the photographs do you recognise? Write brief descriptions of all the ones you are sure about.

a

b

c

d

e

f

g

h

❸ Working in pairs, compare your descriptions. Then try to match each of the photographs above with one below.

What are the connections between them? Check your ideas with other pairs.

1

2

3

4

5

6

7

8

❹ You are going to hear some British sounds. First, close your eyes and try to imagine what they might be and where you would hear them. Then listen again and write down any ideas you have about the sounds.

❺ Check your ideas with a partner. Then fill in as many of the spaces as you can in the <u>first column</u> of the table below.

	Correct answer	Incorrect answer	Clues	Other information
1	tube train			
2		telephone		
3				
4				
5				
6			mechanical tune	
7				
8				
9				British police cars have sirens
10				

❻ Now listen to a group of students discussing the sounds you have just been listening to. While you listen, complete the rest of the table.

AGREEING AND DISAGREEING

❼ Look at these different ways of agreeing and disagreeing. Put them in order from the most to the least direct and from the most to the least polite.

❽ Now look at your new lists. Can you see a connection between them? Which expressions would you use if you were talking to your host family? Or to a close friend? Or another student?

<u>Agreement</u>
Yes, I'm sure you're right.
Yes, that's true.
That's just what I think.
Yes, that's it.
I must say I agree with you.
Yes, I think you're right.
Exactly.

<u>Disagreement</u>
Rubbish!
I'm not sure I agree with you there.
You're absolutely wrong.
I can't go along with that.
That's what you think, is it?
I disagree.
No, I don't think so.

CERTAINTY AND UNCERTAINTY

❾ Look again at the photographs on the opposite page. What else do you know about them? What can you guess? What are you not sure of? Choose appropriate phrases to discuss the photographs.

I'm sure it's .... / No, I'm sure it isn't ....
I think it must be .... / I don't think it can be ....
It's ...., isn't it?
It might be ....
I think it's ....
It could be ....
I'm really not too sure, but maybe it's ....
I don't know ....

SECTION 2

HOW DID YOU GET HERE?

❶ Take a sheet of paper and use the cues below to write briefly about the day when you travelled to Britain. (Don't write your name!) Ask your teacher if you need help.

● Describe the weather on the morning that you left.

● Describe the journey from your front door to the airport, railway station, bus station or border crossing if you came by car.

● List the things that you found most interesting when you arrived.

❷ When you have finished, pass your information sheet to the teacher.

❸ Now take one of the information sheets (not your own!) from the teacher. Correct any mistakes that you see and then try to find the person who wrote it. You must <u>not</u> show your piece of paper until you are sure that you have found its author.

TALKING ABOUT DIFFERENT PLACES IN THE WORLD

The names of countries, people and languages often change slightly from one language to another. The purpose of this activity is to consider how to talk about places, people and cultures in English.

❹ **Whole class discussion:** Work out where <u>everyone</u> in the class comes from. Shade in the country on the world map and mark the city or town with a dot. Then write down the English name for the country and the city or town. Ask the teacher to help check the names and spellings, but the teacher should not be part of the discussion.

❺ **Evaluation:** In pairs, consider the following:

● How well did you explain yourself to the class?
● If you were not sure about what someone said, how did you ask them to clarify?
● Is it more difficult to understand someone who makes some grammatical mistakes or someone who has unusual pronunciation?
● What difficulties do you have when speaking and listening in the class?
● Who controlled the discussion?

❻ <u>QUIZ</u>

1 The class should divide into two groups, A and B. (If the class is larger than about sixteen, then try four groups.) Each group should then write ten statements about places in the world to see whether the other group knows where the country is.

Examples:

● *This country is north of Italy but south of Germany. It is not a member of the European Community. (**Answer**: Switzerland)*

● *There is a huge river running through the north of this large country in South America and its major cities are Rio and Sao Paulo.*

● *English people sometimes call the people from this country 'Kiwis'. It is made up of two large islands and some small ones to the north of Antarctica.*

---

2 Return all of the statements to the teacher, who will manage the quiz using the statements from group A to put to group B and the statements from group B to put to group A. S/he should write the statement on the board and any errors should be corrected first.

3 If the team gets the right answer straight away, then two points are awarded. If the team can't, it may ask a question to help it to get the answer, but then only one point can be awarded.

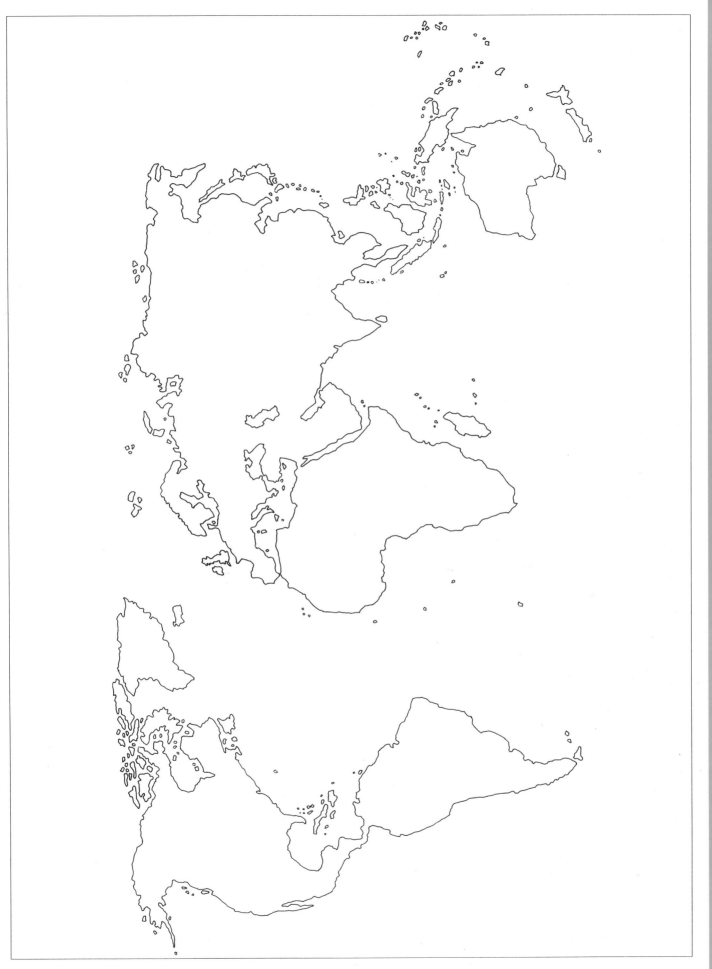

READING

❶ Here is the beginning of the chapter about Great Britain in the *Let's Go: Guide to Europe*. It is divided into four parts. Before you read the text make a list of the sort of information you expect to find in each section.

❷ Now scan the passage to find the information you need to answer the questions at the end. You do not need to read the passage from the beginning through to the end and you do not need to understand every word. (Note that the passage is written in American English so you may notice some differences in spelling and grammar.)

GREAT BRITAIN

GETTING THERE

The cheapest way to reach Britain from continental Europe is to swim the English Channel; this requires extraordinary stamina and has been tackled by only a handful of travelers. Fortunately, many ferries and hovercrafts connect Great Britain with various ports. The most frequent service is from Calais and Boulogne in France to Dover and nearby Folkestone (both about 2 hr. southeast of London by rail); there is also service from Ostend, Dieppe, Le Havre, Cherbourg, Roscoff, Santander, Hamburg, the Hook of Holland, and several Scandinavian ports, as well as Dublin and Rosslare in Ireland. The fare between Calais or Boulogne and Dover is about £20. Ostend-Dover is about the same. The Dover-London rail fare is £14.50; thumbing from Dover to London is quick. Budget-bus deals are often competitive with these prices; coaches originate in Paris, Brussels, and Amsterdam, and continue through to London. Flights to London, especially from Paris, may be economical, but remember to add the cost of transportation from the airport to the city center.

TRANSPORTATION

Rail transport in Great Britain is extensive and expensive: prices outpace most of those on the continent and Eurail is not valid (although InterRail is). British Rail offers a huge and perplexing variety of passes, reductions, and discounts. The best deal is the **Young Person's Railcard**, which gives you a third off any British Rail ticket. The card is valid for an entire year and is available at most rail stations. Supply proof of age (under 24) or student status (ISIC acceptable), plus two photos. Railcards are also available to seniors and for disabled travelers; these cards entitle the holder to discounts of 50% off some fares. Family travelcards can give adults a saving of 33-50%, and children travel for £1. **Intercity Savers,** available to all, are cheap round-trip fares between many large cities, with savings of about 30%.

In British nomenclature one way is 'single,' round-trip is 'return', and 'period return' is a round-trip ticket that must be used within a specified time (usually 30 days).

Express coaches (long-distance buses) are cheaper than trains and often almost as fast. The **National Express/Scottish Citylink** intercity coach network covers most of Britain; a **Student Coach Card** cuts 33% from their already low fares.

Hitchhiking in Great Britain is among Europe's best, since lorry (truck) drivers are always on the road. Solo travelers have the best luck (most lorry cabs are two-seaters); couples, especially a male and a female, should also make time. The best time for finding long rides is early in the morning.

Undoubtedly, the finest way to see Britain is on foot. Villages are usually only a couple of miles apart, and most have one or two places that will put you up for the night.

PRACTICAL INFORMATION

There are independent local tourist offices everywhere in Great Britain; any will book you a room in a bed and breakfast, and most will post a list after closing. Tourist offices are also excellent sources of information on local hiking routes and sights.

There are two breeds of new payphone: those that are coin-operated (10p and 50p) and those that operate with an electronic **Phonecard** (purchased in denominations from £2 to £10 at post offices and newsagents). If the display flashes '999 calls only', find another call box. Rates fall after 6pm. Directory assistance is 192, 142 in London; the operator is 100. **The national emergency number is 999.**

ACCOMMODATIONS AND CAMPING

Hospitable bed and breakfasts are rampant (£8-12, in London £17-20). The British and Scottish Tourist Boards publish *Where to Stay* books. **Tourist Information Centres** in each town can provide a list of accommodations and campsites. They will also find you a room and often book rooms in other towns. Most B&Bs will accept a telephone reservation, but few will keep the room past noon without a deposit. B&Bs are usually grouped together. Usually, if a place is full, the owner will refer you to another establishment. In very small towns, you can ask at the pub or the post office for people offering B&B.

Britain has hundreds of youth hostels, both IYHF and independent. The *England and Wales YHA Guide* and *Scotland YHA Guide* are invaluable for locating official hostels and checking closing dates. Hostel rates, which depend on the traveler's age and the grade of the hostel, hover between £3-5 (higher in London). You must tote an IYHF membership card to stay at affiliated hostels or buy an 'International Guest Card.' These hostels are generally closed from 10am to 5pm, and impose an evening curfew (usually about 11pm). All require sleep sacks, which they sell or rent for a nominal fee. If these regulations cramp your style, stick to looser independent establishments. Always book ahead in high season.

Camping can be a wet proposition any time of the year, but it also gives you the most freedom. British campsites are very civilized, with facilities ranging from flush toilets to lounges. You usually have to put up with an adjacent caravan site. Farmers will frequently let you camp on their land, sometimes for a small fee, but you should always ask before pitching your tent.

Self-catering accommodations are growing in popularity. Flats, cottages, and caravans are rented by the week; they can be economical if you (and friends) plan to stay in one place for a while. The tourist office has a list of these in each town.

*B&B = 'Bed and Breakfast'

1 How much is the passenger fare to cross the English Channel from Calais to Dover?
2 How much does Bed and Breakfast outside London cost?
3 How much discount can you get off the cost of coach travel with a Student Coach Card?
4 Where can you buy a Phonecard?
5 What is the emergency number in Great Britain if you need the fire brigade, the police or the ambulance service?
6 What time do most British Youth Hostels lock their doors at night?

❸ Although we do not always know all of the words in a reading passage, we can often make a 'good guess'. Here are some sentences taken from the passage. Choose the definition which you think fits the meaning of the word that has been underlined.

1 Swimming the English Channel requires extraordinary stamina.

   a interest and love
   b skill and power
   c strength and energy

2 Eurail is not valid though InterRail is.

   a able to be used
   b very useful
   c very common

3 Directory assistance is 192, 142 in London.

   a the telephone number to ring if you want to know how to use the phone
   b the telephone number to ring if you have a complaint
   c the telephone number to ring if you want to find someone's number

4 Tourist Information Centres in each town can provide a list of accommodations and campsites, will find you a room and often book rooms in other towns.

   a tell you the address of places to stay in other towns
   b make reservations for you to stay in other towns
   c tell you about the quality of accommodation in other towns.

❹ Work in pairs. There may still be some words in the passage that you are not certain about. Skim the passage together and underline those words which you do not know. Then look at the words again. Choose eight that you think are more important and find out what they mean. When you have finished, compare the eight that you have chosen with those of another pair.

❺ Imagine that you are preparing a tourist guide. What are the pictures of Britain that you would like to include? Write down the descriptions for three more scenes that you would like to include.

❻ Circulate the descriptions for everyone in the class to read. If you see any mistakes in the writing, show the authors and then correct them. Which are the most popular pictures of Britain?

SECTION 4

LANGUAGE STUDY

TENSE REVIEW

❶ Past tenses

Read the extracts below and write the name of the tense of the verbs used beside the extract. The first one has been done for you.

The island had been invaded by the Romans and the Vikings before the Norman French....   *past perfect*

Under Queen Victoria 'Britannia ruled the waves' and the sun never set on the British Empire, etc., etc.; then the two World Wars destroyed both the Empire and much of that social inequality.   _____

Mrs Thatcher was attending a European Community Ministers' summit meeting in 1990 when....   _____

The British people had been happily using solid red public telephone boxes for many years and then.....   _____

❷ Time words

Complete the following sentences using *before, after, until* or *ago*.

1 The first time I came to England was four years _____

2 _____ I came to England I went on a short English course in my home town.
3 The house seemed so empty _____ they had left.
4 I waited _____ six o'clock and then I went home.

❸ Linking events in the past

Combine these pairs of sentences using *because*. Change one of the simple past tense forms into the past perfect.

Example: *I stayed at the party until midnight.*
                I missed the last bus home.

I missed the last bus home *because* I had stayed at the party until midnight. *or*
Because I had stayed at the party until midnight, I missed the last bus home.

1 I spent too much while I was on holiday.
   I could not afford to repair my car.

_____

2 I ate and drank too much at the party.
   I felt terrible in the morning.

_____

3 I did not manage to prepare for the project very well.
   I left all my notes at school.

_____

4 Peter left Mary.
   Mary fell in love with James.

_____

❹ Non-past tenses

Read the extracts below and write the name of the tense of the verbs used beside the extract. The first one has been done for you.

The cheapest way to reach Britain from Continental Europe is to swim the English Channel; this requires extraordinary stamina....   *present simple*

Each group that has come has shaken and refigured the kaleidoscope of cultures; Celts, Saxons, Angles, Jutes, Danes, Normans, Irish, Scots, Welsh, Flemings, Huguenots, Jews, Africans, West Indians, Pakistanis and Indians – all have contributed to the British peoples.   _____

Self-catering accommodation is growing in popularity; flats, cottages and caravans....   _____

Tourism in Britain has been steadily growing throughout the second half of this century.   _____

❺ Time words

Complete the following sentences using *for, since, never, already* and *yet*.

1 I have _____ been to Edinburgh, but I know London quite well.
2 Sarah's husband is French, but he has been living in Britain _____ twelve years.
3 I have wanted to go and watch an English cricket match _____ I was eleven.
4 They have finished this exercise _____, it must be too easy.
5 Wait for Simone, she has not finished _____.

❻ Imagine a situation where one student is questioning another about studying English. Write down the questions that might have produced these responses and complete the dialogue.

_____

English, oh, about eleven years now.

_____

When I was about eight, in primary school.

_____

It is difficult to say what level I am. Sometimes it is quite easy to understand the people here and sometimes I think I cannot understand anything at all. I suppose I am what they call an intermediate-level student.

_____

Well I need to improve my listening skills, certainly, and I suppose I should spend more time learning vocabulary.

_____

Oh yes, I'm really enjoying it. The teachers are friendly, I like the town and I have fallen in love. The course is great.

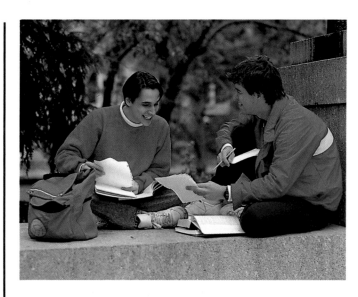

❼ Working in pairs, use some of the ideas in Exercise 6 and write down ten questions you would like to ask. When you have finished, join with another pair and share your ideas. As a group of four, decide which ten questions you would like to use.

❽ Draw lines across to match the grammar statements with the examples that support them.

Statements

Simple past tenses report completed actions.

Present perfect tenses relate time past to time present.

The simple present tense can be used to talk about things that are always true.

Ago combines with simple past tenses.

Since combines with perfect tense forms.

The past progressive tense can be used to describe an incomplete past action.

The present progressive tense can be used to talk about the future.

Examples

I have been studying English for three years.

The sun rises in the east and sets in the west.

I arrived in England a week ago and I'm staying for one month.

The telephone was ringing.

I am flying to Glasgow on Friday.

I climbed the stairs and then I went to bed.

I haven't seen her since Friday.

❾ Writing your own grammar notebook

Working in groups of four, use the headings on the right to write your own grammar notes. Write down your own rules and provide example sentences. Use a good grammar book and ask your teacher when you are not sure. Diagrams to show the relationship between different time periods are useful.

Present Simple	Past Simple
Present Progressive	Past Progressive
Present Perfect	Past Perfect
Present Perfect Progressive	Past Perfect Progressive

SECTION 5

SPEAKING

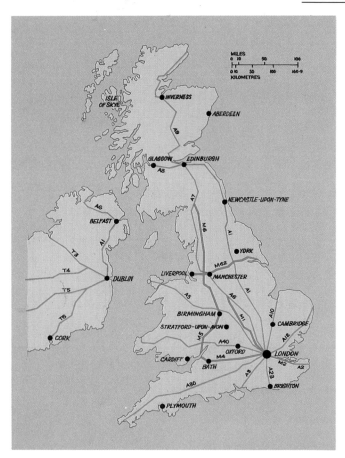

❶ Working in pairs, look at the map of Britain. Where are you? How many of the places have you been to? Where would you like to go to? Why?

❷ Now join with another pair and share your ideas.

❸ You have a free weekend (Friday night until Monday morning), a comfortable car and enough money. As a group of four, decide how you would like to spend your weekend. Plan your journey, decide how you will spend your time, where you will stay overnight and what you expect to see. Prepare to tell the rest of the class.

❹ You will hear six people talking about where they come from. Some may sound strange. Listen to them to find out where they come from. Make a note on the map.

READING

Inside out

Gosia Furlong (right) is Polish and has lived in London for three years.

What do you most like about the British?
They make an effort to be friendly in any circumstances.

What do you most dislike about them?
Their ability to watch snooker on television for hours on end.

What do you most respect about them?
Their tolerance.

What do you think about the way they conduct their love affairs?
They seem to be successful in their conquests. In Poland we think of them as being cold and unapproachable but it is just a stereotype.

What do you think of British television?
Boring. Polish television is better, more choice (especially in films and plays) and there is less canned laughter.

What do you think of British television?
They are a bit obsessed with murder and crime. In Poland they prefer politics.

And the British sense of humour?
Subtle, intelligent and — thinking of Spitting Image — vicious.

In what way is Britain better than Poland?
The telephones work better and economics make more sense here.

And how is Poland better than Britain?
I would rather bring children up in Poland.

How would you rate the following (on a scale of 1 to 10)? *Style:* 9. *Promptness of plumbers/repair men:* 7. *Public transport:* 0. *Road manners:* 9. *Politeness:* 10.

❺ On 17 January 1992 the *Guardian* newspaper printed these comments made by a Polish woman as she talked about the British. After you have considered Gosia's comments, read the multiple-choice task and choose the answer which you think fits best.

1   Generally, Gosia

  a   dislikes the British and their television.
  b   seems to like the British but doesn't think much of their television.
  c   thinks that the British are unfriendly, cold and unapproachable.
  d   prefers living in Britain to living in Poland.

2   According to Gosia, the British

  a   have good road manners and excellent public transport.
  b   are unsuccessful lovers, but their repair men arrive on time.
  c   are polite and tolerant.
  d   try to be friendly, but are always thinking about murder and crime.

3   British television

  a   does not have many programmes for children.
  b   is full of programmes about politics.
  c   has a lot of boring comedy programmes.
  d   consists of hours and hours of snooker and nothing else.

❻ Now find the adjectives in the passage which fit the definitions below:

  a   clever but with an intelligence that is not easily noticed
  b   allowing others to behave in a way that you may not like without getting angry
  c   dangerous and likely to cause pain
  d   always thinking about the same thing
  e   difficult to speak to, unfriendly

❼ The same questions were given to another person, Branka, who comes from Yugoslavia and has lived in and out of Britain with British people for ten years.

Working in pairs, read her responses and underline those comments which seem to agree with Gosia. Put a cross beside those comments which seem to reveal a different impression of the British.

What do you most like about the British?

Their tradition and the way they

enjoy things from the past.

What do you most dislike about them?

Fair skin and red noses.

What do you most respect about them?

Their sense of justice.

What do you think about the way they conduct their love affairs?

I suppose they must know what they are

doing, but it is certainly very private.

What do you think of British television?

It is seasonal and changes like the weather.

American and Australian rubbish cannot be

compared with a good crime series like

'Inspector Morse' or 'Poirot'.

And the British sense of humour?

Apart from some television comedians, the

British are not very funny unless you have

a taste for irony and bitter humour.

I have learned it.

In what way is Britain better than your country?

My country does not exist any more.

And how is your country better than Britain?

It is certainly never boring.

How would you rate the following (on a scale of 1 to 10)?

Style: _7_

Promptness of plumbers/repair men: _9_

Public transport: _2½_

Road manners: _8_

Politeness: _8_

WRITING

❽ Now explain what you think about the British. Write down your own responses on a separate sheet of paper.

VOCABULARY

❶ Storing and organising new words.

Working in pairs, think about new words you have found this week. Which words were 'new' to you? How do you store them? List the techniques that you both use.

❷ Active and passive vocabulary.

Choose five words that you have found this week and discuss the following:

1 Do you think you will often need to write the word?
2 Can you say the word correctly?
3 Will you recognise the word when you read it again?
4 Will you understand if someone uses the word in conversation?
5 Do you remember the sentence or expression where you found it? Do you know what type of word it is? (Noun, adjective, adverb, verb etc.)
6 Do you know how the word works? (For example: if it is a verb can you use it in different tense forms? If it is an adjective, does it have a noun form e.g. happy > happiness? If it is an adverb, what is the adjective form, e.g. quickly > quick?)

❸ Word sets, synonyms (words with a similar meaning) and antonyms (words with an opposite meaning).

Now choose another five words that have been new to you this week.

1 Can you associate them with any other words?
2 Are there any other words that have a similar meaning?
3 Are there any words with an opposite meaning?

❹ Look at the pages taken from students' vocabulary notebooks. Do you use any of the techniques here? How useful are they? Reconsider the ten words that you have chosen from this week's study. Could you use any of these techniques to help you?

❺ Try some of these techniques for yourself. Take the topics TELEPHONING and TRAVEL IN BRITAIN. How could you store and organise words around these topics?

❻ Exercises in textbooks can also be helpful when you are learning new vocabulary or activating words that you already know. Try these.

1 Which is the 'odd man out' in the word sets below?

  – *friendly, approachable, pleasant, agreeable, difficult*
  – *clever, intelligent, dull, sharp, bright*
  – *policeman, lawyer, criminal, judge, fireman*
  – *yawn, ache, pain, hurt, cramp*
  – *snooker, billiards, skittles, darts, pool*

2 Match the words on the left with those words and expressions that have a similar meaning on the right.

prefer   victory
polite   hitch-hiking
tradition   round-trip
single   history
promptness   would rather
relaxed   well-mannered
thumbing   one-way
return   buy
fare   easy-going
hospitable   swiftness
purchase   welcoming
conquest   situation
circumstance cost

3 Read the following extract and choose from the words below to fill the gaps.

One of the strangest things about the British is the way that they always seem to enjoy talking about the

_____. They probably talk about the weather because it is always changing. You can get up

in the morning and face a wonderful _____ sunny summer's day. There isn't a cloud in the sky, so off you go to work with your shirt-sleeves rolled up and

a _____ on your face. The air is warm

but not hot and a gentle _____ moves softly through the trees. At lunch-time you come out of the office and think of going for a walk in the

_____ and finding a quiet spot to eat your sandwiches. A quick look back to the office. 'No,' you think to yourself, 'I don't need the umbrella.' Then just as you sit down there is a gentle rumble then a crack of thunder. The wind gets up and it all begins. The

heavens open and it _____ it down. Rain, rain, rain. It bounces off the tarmac paths

and _____ off into the flowerbeds.

It is no wonder that the _____ in England is so green. Back to the office, drenched. 'Oh, you got caught in it too, did you?' as you drip in the lift.

'It's still _____ it down outside.'
'Raining cats and dogs.' 'Fine weather for

_____.' And everyone is happy because they can talk about it.

chucks ducks bucketing bright weather smile soaks park breeze grass

4 Talking about the weather.

Task: In small groups, choose one of the following headwords. Prepare a poster display to include and show the meaning of all the words that the group can associate with the headword. When you have finished, display the poster. Use dictionaries, drawings, illustrations from magazines, etc.

Headwords: RAIN   WIND   SNOW   SUN

PROJECT - A TOWN PORTRAIT

Your class is going to produce a portrait – in words and pictures – of the town (or area of the city) where you are studying. Your project will be read/seen by other students in your school.

STAGE ONE: Preparation and research

You will need a lot of background information in order to select the things which interest you. Your teacher – and other people in the school – will certainly be able to help, but first you must decide what you want to find out and how you are going to do it.

1 Work in groups. What do you already know about the town? What did you know before you arrived? What have you discovered since your arrival? Think about the following:

- history
- legends/stories
- industry/economy
- special traditions

Share the information you have and think about the things you would like to find out. Make a list of questions you want to ask. Here are some examples:

- What do people in other parts of the country think of the town/city – and of its inhabitants?
- Is the town/city famous for any reason?
- Is there any typical local food or drink?

Add your own ideas and then compare your questions with other groups.

3 Think about where you can go and who you can ask to get the information you need.

Examples:
- school library
- town library
- Tourist Information Centre
- teachers
- host family
- local shopkeepers

Decide which groups are going to be responsible for different areas of research. Then in each group, decide on the best way to divide the work. For example, who is going to organise interviews? Who is going to look up information in the library? Who is going to contact local companies?

Finally, what resources will you need? Notebook? Camera? Cassette recorder? Other?

2 Put your questions into groups, using as many headings as you need. Here are some possible sets of headings:

- PAST
- PEOPLE
- SHOPPING

PRESENT
PLACES
LEISURE

FUTURE
PRODUCTS
TOURISM

14

STAGE TWO: Planning and editing

You now need to organise the information you have collected and to think about how you are going to present it.

1 Form editorial groups to collect information under your main headings.

Examples:

Main heading: THE PAST
Groups: ancient history
              pre-20th century
              early 20th century
              post-war

Main heading: TOURISM
Groups: hotels
              tourist attractions
              twin towns/special contacts
              information and services

2 Editorial tasks:

a Make sure that you can understand the notes/texts/transcripts of interviews brought to you. If anything is unclear, ask the writer(s) to explain what they wanted to say.

b Decide what information is essential. Is the text too long? Are some facts/ideas repeated? Are there some things which will be more/less interesting to your readers? If you want to cut anything, ask for permission from the writer(s).

c Are the facts/ideas in the text presented in the best possible order? Again, if you want to make any changes, ask for the writer's permission.

d Look out for any mistakes of spelling, punctuation and grammar.

STAGE THREE: Presentation

With the help of your teacher, you must now decide on the best way to present your Town Portrait. You should select a method of presentation which will make your project easily available to other students. Discuss the advantages and disadvantages of these possibilities:

● a photocopied 'magazine' – number of copies? to be sold or given away?
● a wall display – where everyone can see it
● a loose-leaf file – other students could add their own information
● a 'mixed media' presentation - using audio/video recordings, overhead projector, readings etc.
● other?

REVIEW

PROJECT EVALUATION

❶ Was your project successful? Think about your working methods as well as the final product.

Preparation and research
What do you think of the questions that you asked? Did they help you to get the information you wanted? How useful were the general headings you chose? Did you discover other headings later on? Did you go to the right people/places to get information? Did you record the information clearly?

Planning and editing
How easy/difficult was the task of editing? What kinds of corrections/changes did you have to make? How did the writers react to your suggestions? What advice would you give to another editorial group?

Presentation
Are you satisfied with the results of your project? Does it contain enough information about the topics you have chosen? Is it easy to understand? How could you improve it?

THINKING ABOUT LANGUAGE LEARNING

Many people believe that you can become a more efficient learner of another language if you give yourself time to think about your learning experience. This means thinking about your needs as a learner, your particular strengths and weaknesses and the way that you study.

❷ In small groups, discuss questions 1-3 in each section below. Write questions 4-7 using the prompts, then write three more questions to complete the questionnaire.

Section 1: The Language Learning Experience in General

1 In addition to English, have you ever studied any other foreign languages?

2 Do you think you are good at learning languages?

3 How long have you been learning English?

4 Why/English?

5 England/before?

6 listen/read in English?

7 listen? _____

8 _____

9 _____

10 _____

Section 2: Studying English

1 While you are in England, which language skills do you expect to develop?

2 Which books have you used to study English in your own country?

3 What is different about studying in England?

4 most useful/this book?

5 grammar and correction?

6 speaking and fluency work?

7 vocabulary?_____

8 _____

9 _____

10 _____

What sort of learner are you?

1 Do you worry about speaking, in case you make a mistake?

2 Do you enjoy working in pairs or in small groups?

_____

3 Do you want the teacher to spend more time explaining grammar rules?

_____

4 studying on your own?

_____

5 talking to strangers?

_____

6 learning new words?

_____

7 listening to radio and watching television?

_____

8 _____

9 _____

10 _____

❸ Now use your questionnaire to interview two other people in the class. Try to choose someone who is much older or younger than you are or someone who is learning English for reasons that are quite different from yours.

❹ When you have finished, return to your groups. Discuss your findings and identify one issue that you have found particularly interesting and report it back to the rest of the class.

❺ Discussion

How do the students in your class feel about English? What patterns are there? What are the common problems? What do most people expect from the course?

READING

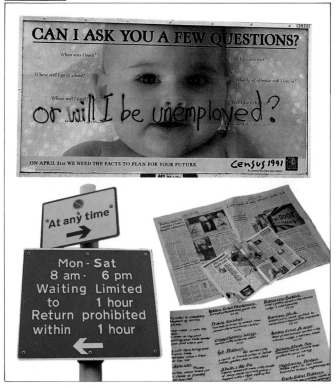

❻ In pairs, make a list of all the things that you read in English yesterday and today.

❼ Sort your list into groups by identifying situations where
   a you needed to read from start to finish and understand every word.
   b you just needed to get that general idea or understand the topic.
   c you were reading for particular information.

❽ What problems do you have (if any) with reading in each of the situations above?

❾ Were you sure about why you were reading in each of the situations?

❿ How do you guess the meaning of words that you do not know?

REVIEW

⓫ While you are in Britain it is a good idea to keep a learner diary to record and evaluate your experiences. Use the following prompts to begin your diary.

In this unit I have learned ....

The things I found easy were ....

I would like more practice of ....

I really enjoyed .... because ....

⓬ Think of someone you know whose English is slightly better than yours and write her/him a letter telling your experiences this week. You may wish to include the following:

● a report on your journey to Britain
● a description of where you are living
● your thoughts about the school and your class
● what you think you are learning
● what you like about the British
● what you have found to be funny about life in Britain
● your hopes for the next few weeks.

❶ Look carefully at each photograph. Where is it? Write down all the words that you associate with each place.

❷ Where would you choose to go? List your top five leisure activities in order of preference. (If you prefer, you can include other locations not shown in the photographs.)

a

b

c

d

e

f

g

h

❸ You are going to hear some sounds. Where do they come from? While you listen, match the sounds with the photographs.

❹ Now listen to these three extracts. While you listen, make notes in the table below. The first one has been started for you.

	1	2	3
Location	Restaurant		
Relationship between speakers	Waiter/customer		
Tone of voice (casual/formal)	Polite, very formal		
Purpose	Settling the bill		
Interesting expressions			
Other information			

❺ Working with a partner, compare the notes you have made, then listen again and decide whether these statements are TRUE or FALSE.

1 The couple were pleased with their meal and ate ham for the main course.
2 The restaurant does not accept payment by credit card.
3 The couple did not realise how late it was.

4 Steve drank orange juice and lemonade.
5 They order plain crisps.
6 They plan to spend the whole evening in the pub.

7 They want tickets for the evening performance.
8 They don't want to sit high up in the balcony.
9 They will pay for the tickets when they arrive at the theatre.

PLACING AN ORDER

❻ Look at these expressions. Put them in order from the most to the least direct, and from the most polite to the least polite.

a Er – I wonder if you have any seats for Tuesday evening?
b A *Sunday Express* and a box of matches.
c Hello, we are ready to order now.
d I want to speak to the manager!
e Give us a chocolate, Steve.
f Could you possibly let me have a table for two on Saturday night?
g I wonder if you might be able to help me. I'm looking for any early porcelain by . . .
h Standing room only, it doesn't matter. Give us three tickets.

❼ Where do you think you might hear the expressions? What do you think is the relationship between the speaker and the listener?

❽ Now, working with a partner, choose *one* of the expressions and use it as part of a short dialogue that develops the situation. Act out the situation to the rest of the class.

SECTION 2–ANYONE FOR TENNIS?

❶ All around the world, sport is an important part of our leisure. You can tell a lot about the people of a country by watching the games they play. Obviously, different countries may have many sports in common but the style of play is often very different. Take football as a good example:

Working with a partner, write down the names of all the sports you can think of. How many have you played?

❷ Here are some images from popular British games and sports. Look at the pictures. Can you name them? Can you play them? Do you know the rules?

❸ Here are some of the letters from the names of the games and sports here. Can you complete them?

t . . . . s   b . . . s

f . . h . . g   g . . f

s . . . . . r   f l

d . . . n . . s   c . . . k . t

a . . . . . y   s . . . . . . s

c . . q . . t   d . . . s

t . . . . . g the c . . . r

h . . . . r . . . . g

f . x h . . . . . g

r . . . . g

❹ Think about the games and sports again. Write down five questions that you want to ask.

❺ Working in groups of four, share your questions and then use them to make a *new* list of five questions to ask the rest of the class.

❻ **Discussion.** 'Games and sports may tell us a lot about the men of each country but they don't tell us much about the women.' How far do you agree with this statement?

READING

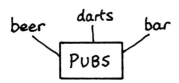

❶ Brainstorm as many words as you can which are connected with pubs and add them to the spidergram.

❷ How much do you know about pubs? Decide whether the following statements are TRUE or FALSE *before* you read the text.

1 There are more pubs in Scotland than in England.
2 You can find English pubs all over the world.
3 Young people under the age of 18 are not allowed to enter a pub.
4 The majority of pub customers are men.
5 The *King's Head* is the most popular name for an English pub.

❸ Now scan the text quickly to check your answers.

THE ENGLISH PUB – A Unique Institution

The pub is an institution unique to England, and there is nothing more English. It is not an American bar, darkened still by the long shadow of Prohibition*; not a French café, where people sunnily drink apéritifs on the pavement; not a Bavarian beer-hall, full of swaying and noise. Other countries have royal families, parliaments, and double-decker buses, but only England has pubs. In New York and Tokyo, Hamburg and Paris, Turin and Zurich, there are 'pubs' called the *Britannia*, the *Sir Winston Churchill* and suchlike, but they are not English. The pub has never been successfully transplanted into other countries, because it is an organic part of the growth of English community life. It has only half-heartedly spread beyond the Black Mountains to

Wales and the Cheviot Hills to Scotland – and, in spite of Dublin's claims, has hardly bothered to cross the sea to Ireland. But when England presents itself to the world at large, the image usually includes a pub.

The pub at its best may be a place for drinking and talking (or, better still, for talking and drinking), but it can also be a place for eating, for games and sports, for music (jukebox or live, all tastes catered for) or for theatre. It can be any of these things, or a little of each, so long as it remains a pub. To be a pub, it must cater for those people who want nothing more than a drink; it must serve them at regular prices, and without charging for entry.

The pub enters the consciousness of the Englishman years before *he* can enter the pub. (Unless the pub has a special place for children – the few that do are likely to advertise the fact – the house cannot admit anyone under 14, nor serve anyone under 18.) The pub is a landmark in conversation: something happened outside the *Rose and Crown*; turn left at the *King Charles*; park your car 100 yards past the *Star and Garter*. Pub is a three-letter word that serves so many purposes. The pub is the place where lights shine through translucent glass in the evenings, the doors swing open to exhale noisy conversation and beery smells. The pub is the place where stubble-chinned schoolboys sneak in plain clothes to prove their manliness; anyone can fool around with girls, but only real men drink in pubs. The machismo of the pub has mercifully subsided, though it is still primarily a male domain. Few women would hesitate to go into a pub if they had arranged to meet a man friend there, but many would shrink from drinking there alone.

Pub signs

Other lands have names for their bars or cafés, but not quite like the English names. Other lands have tavern signs of a kind, but the English variety is unique in its extent and range, its imagination and colour.

When the University of East Anglia opened its own pub, a competition was organised to establish a name for it.

The students refused to stretch their minds and for a number of years the pub was called *The Pub!* There are more than 400 *King's Heads* in England, 300 *Queen's Heads* and 1,000 *Crowns*, making the last the most popular pub name. The most appropriately-named pub in England must be the *Adam and Eve* in the village of Paradise in Gloucestershire. The longest name was *The Thirteenth Mounted Cheshire Rifleman Inn* at Stalybridge, near Manchester, until it was shortened by the removal of the soldier from his horse. Now that he is no longer 'Mounted', the longest pub name is *The London, Chatham and Dover Railway Tavern*. The strangest name may be that of a pub in Devon, where a seventeenth-century landlord was a solitary drinker who used to rebuff customers by shouting that there was nobody in. The pub was eventually renamed the *Nobody Inn!*

When the comedian, Ted Ray, used to mention the *Frog and Nightgown* in his radio show, did any listener need to be told that he was talking about a pub? (There is at least one such house, in London's Old Kent Road.) Which visitor to England has not looked out for the *Pig and Whistle*? (One *Pig and Whistle* in Norwich has jokingly been misnamed by its customers for so long that the landlord has actually changed its name to the *Wig and Pistle*!)

(*Adapted from Michael Jackson, The English Pub, New Burlington Books 1976*)

> *NOTE - Prohibition: the period during the 1920s in the USA when the sale of alcohol was illegal.

❹ Match each of the following words from the text with the correct meaning on the right.

swaying	letting light shine through
transplanted	moving from side to side
organic	refuse
half-heartedly	become smaller
cater	moved to a different place
regular	normal
translucent	without enthusiasm
exhale	breathe out
subsided	be unwilling to
domain	natural
shrink from	territory
rebuff	provide

❺ Complete the following sentences *in your own words,* using ideas from the text.

1 English 'pubs' in other countries never succeed in being real English pubs because _____

_____

_____

2 English pubs may be very different from each other, but they all _____

_____

_____

3 Englishmen feel at home in the pub, whereas Englishwomen _____

_____

_____

PLAYING THE GAME

Two of the most popular pub games are darts and dominoes. Can anyone in the class explain how these games are played?

❻ Descriptions of darts and dominoes have been mixed up in the following paragraph. Work out which sentences belong to each game and rewrite the two descriptions.

It comes from archery and today's players still talk about arrows. It has become the most popular of all pub games. The game was played by the Ancient Chinese, and spread into Europe via Italy. It was introduced to Britain by French prisoners-of-war in the early nineteenth century. In the basic game each player has a set number of pieces (usually six or seven). Each player throws three times. The standard English game is based on a scoring system which descends from 301. To start, whoever has the 'double six' has to put it down. It is possible to start with 401, 501 or even 1,001 points. To start you have to hit the narrow outside band on the board, which counts as a double. The players put down their pieces alternately, always matching their piece with one already on the table, which has the same number of white spots. In a simple game, the winner is the first person to get rid of all his/her pieces. It is possible to adopt an entirely different set of rules while using the standard board. In a standard game, the winner must reach exactly zero with another 'double'! The skill of the game lies in reducing as quickly as possible the numerical value of your pieces, while working out – and memorising – the contents of your opponent's hand!

❼ Compare your two descriptions with a partner. What were the words which helped you to separate the two games?

❽ Think of a game that you know well. Do you know how/where it started? Where do people play it? How many people can take part? What equipment do you need to play? What do the players have to do? What is the scoring system? How do you win (or lose)? Write a short description of the game, like this :

The game began _____
It is usually played in _____
_____ is a game for two or more _____
It is played with _____
To start, you must _____
Each player must try to _____
If a player _____ then _____
The object of the game is to _____
The winner/loser is the first player to _____
The skill of the game lies in _____

SECTION 4

LANGUAGE STUDY

A

KEEPER'S COUSIN CRUNCHED BY CROCODILE

B

New bank takeover planned

C

© Copyright 1992. Neither the whole, nor any part of the information contained in this manual may be adapted or reproduced in any material form except with the prior written approval of t...

D

Congratulations! You have been carefully selected to take part in this month's lucky draw. A thorough survey has been carried out by our new computer and you have been chosen from a list of some sixty thousand householders to take part in

E

TEA
PRODUCE OF CHINA

G

PURE LAMBSWOOL

Made in Great Britain

F

In the first stage of purification the water is filtered through a layer of coarse sand. In the second stage the process is repeated with the water being passed over a finer grade of sand.

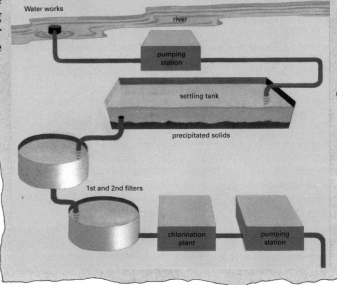

Water works
river
pumping station
settling tank
precipitated solids
1st and 2nd filters
chlorination plant
pumping station

❶ Identify each of these texts.

Where do you think it comes from?
Who wrote it?
Who is it written for?
Is it a beginning, a middle, an end, or a complete text?

Underline the passive verb forms.

ACTIVE OR PASSIVE?

❷ Read the pairs of sentences below. Can you separate them into two groups?

1 The game was played by the Ancient Chinese.
2 The Ancient Chinese played the game.

3 It must cater for those people.
4 Those people must be catered for.

5 The house cannot admit anyone under fourteen.
6 No-one under fourteen can be admitted.

7 For a number of years the pub was called *The Pub*.
8 We called it *The Pub* for a number of years.

9 In the standard English game, you start with 301 and go down .
10 The standard English game is based on a scoring system which descends from 301.

11 Payment by credit card is accepted.
12 We accept payment by credit card.

13 All the seats have been sold.
14 They have sold all the seats.

24

❸ Read these statements about the passive and find the example sentences that are used to explain them. The first one has been done for you.

a. - Passive sentences are formed by combining subject + verb *to be* + past participle.

b. - Changing the tense of the verb *to be* changes the tense of the passive sentence.

c. - Newspaper headlines often use passive sentences (it saves space and gives the idea of formality).

d. - Official, impersonal and legal writing often uses the passive form.

e. - The passive form is used to describe a process. In this case, it is often more important to know what happens than who or what is responsible.

❹ Working in pairs, reconsider the statements. For each statement, find or write another example sentence.

---

will be
* The football match is being shown live on television.
was

* GOVERNMENT MINISTER (IS) FORCED TO RESIGN.

* This book (SUBJECT) was (VERB *to be*) printed (PAST PARTICIPLE) in Hong Kong.

* The document is fed into the fax machine face down. It is then passed over a fluorescent tube - which bounces light off the paper and the image is reflected on to a lens.

* This cover note is issued subject to the terms and conditions within the contract.

LANGUAGE PRACTICE

❺ Read these passive sentences. Can you name the tense form? Can you draw time lines to explain what time that is being referred to?

Now

Past ◄──────────────► Future

1 This watch is made in Switzerland.
2 The classroom is being used this evening.
3 The pub was built on the site of a fourteenth-century hostelry.
4 The musicians were being called to play an encore when the fire began.
5 This year's darts final has been won by Eric again.
6 The school canteen is going to be expanded and will be kept open longer in the evening.

❻ **Impersonal forms.** Certain reporting verbs can be used in the passive voice. Make sentences from the prompts, using the model subject + passive reporting verb + *to* + infinitive.

Example: President/think/leave the country
The president (*subject*) is thought (*passive reporting verb*) to have left (to + *infinitive*) the country.

1 serious fighting/report/broken out/on the border
2 Queen/say/be/one of the world's richest women
3 annual profits/estimate/fall/this year/by about 40%
4 Prime Minister/expect/announce/date of election/this afternoon
5 before his accident/Michael/think/be/one of the best athletes/in the country

❼ **Using *it* to begin an impersonal passive sentence.** Make passive sentences that begin with *it*, using the prompts below.

Example: believe/he/be/elected Chairman
It is believed that he will be elected Chairman.

1 prove/too much salt in the diet/be/bad for you
2 understand/complete European integration/be/not possible
3 agree/she/be/best teacher in the school
4 rumour/Buckingham Palace/be/for sale
5 consider/likely/that/interest rates/fall/next month

❽ Reconsider the sentences you made in Exercises 6 and 7 above. Try to make them active sentences. How does the meaning change?

❾ **Modal verbs in passive constructions.** Convert the sentences below, using a modal verb + the passive.

Example: In the past, it *wasn't possible to provide* free health care.
In the past, free health care *couldn't be provided.*

1 It is essential to maintain high quality free health care.
High quality free health care . . . .
2 It is possible to use salt to clean a wound.
Salt . . . .
3 In some countries it is advisable to boil the drinking water.
In some countries the drinking water . . . .
4 The nurse will probably sort you out quite quickly.
You . . .

25

LEISURE AND ENTERTAINMENT

❶ A recent survey asked more than 1000 people how they liked to spend their leisure time. Can you guess what the results were? Before you read the newspaper article below, place the following leisure pursuits in what you think is their order of popularity in Britain today.

● going to the cinema
● eating out (i.e. going to restaurants)
● sport
● entertaining at home (i.e. inviting friends to dinner)

● going to the theatre
● DIY (= 'Do It Yourself', i.e. home decoration etc.)
● gardening

❷ Use the information from the newspaper article to complete the table below.

❸ What do you think a similar survey would find in your country? How do you like to relax when you are at home? Have you been doing similar things in Britain? Have you tried anything new? Working in groups, find out what other students in the class like doing.

❹ Working in pairs, find the words which belong together and put them into groups. (Some words may belong to more than one group.) Compare your ideas with another pair and use a dictionary to decide about any differences.

theatre, exhibition, concert hall, film, performance, cinema, gallery, concert, screen, museum, orchestra, thriller, stage, audience, soloist, paintings, comedy, play, museum, musicians, box office, sculpture, drama, show, conductor, drawings, musical, director, recital, performer, producer, programme, players, works, pictures

❺ Group the events (a) – (p) under the following headings: *concerts   exhibitions   films   plays   jazz   folk music*

Eastern Daily Press, Monday, May 4, 1992

ONLY ONE IN THREE DO IT THEMSELVES!

Nearly one in three people regards DIY as a leisure pursuit in the same league as watching TV or reading, according to a survey today.

Reaching for the toolbox or paintbrush is marginally more popular than sport when it comes to using leisure time.

Watching TV or videos was the most popular way to relax, with 67 per cent of the survey of over 1000 people saying a slump in front of the television set was one of the three leisure pursuits on which they spent most time.

Reading was the next most popular way to spend leisure time with a score of 46 per cent, followed by gardening (44 per cent) and then DIY, entertaining at home, or eating and drinking outside the home, which all scored 28 per cent. But 30 per cent of men and 21 per cent of women said they found DIY jobs enjoyable.

Sport scored 27 per cent in the leisure league table. Cinema and theatre rated 11 per cent.

Activity	Order of popularity	Percentage
—	1	—
—	2	—
—	—	44%
DIY	—	—
—	—	28%
entertaining	—	—
sport	—	27%
—	6	—

PROOF (15)
Fri 15 May, 5.30pm
Cinema City
A psychological thriller about a blind photographer whose pictures are a kind of proof of the world he cannot see. With its eloquent handling of an original theme, *Proof* must be among the finest films of 1991.
(a)

THE DOROTHEA HARE YOUNG MUSICIANS CONCERT
Mon 11 May, 7.30pm
Lecture Theatre 1, UEA
The programme will include works by Beethoven, Martineau, Chopin and Bach. It is the tenth of a series of annual concerts endowed by the family of the late Dorothea Hare. The object of the series is to give help and encouragement to young performers who have connections with UEA. (Tickets are free of charge).
(b)

JIMMY WITHERSPOON
Fri 29 May, 8pm
UEA Lower Common Room
Making a rare visit to the UK, one of the best jazz and blues singers of our time with a five-piece line-up.
(c)

NORWICH CLASSIC CONCERT
Sun 17 May
Earlham Park
The London Philharmonic Orchestra top the bill in this all-day musical spectacular with a feast of music, lasers and fireworks.
(d)

RESTLESS SHADOWS
Until Sun 3 May
Sainsbury Centre for Visual Arts, UEA
Nine contemporary Japanese sculptors explore a diverse range of striking and innovative compositions, which often bring together brightly coloured soft materials with metal, wood and mixed media.
(e)

□ **JAMES DODDS**
Sat 2 May to Sun 14 June
The Room Upstairs, Christchurch Mansion
An exhibition of prints and paintings by the established Suffolk artist, James Dodds. This exhibition brings together his acclaimed illustrations to George Crabbe's poem, *Peter Grimes*, along with other works influenced by the Suffolk landscapes, his experiences of the sea and his love of boats.

(f)

□ **CONTEMPORARY JEWELLERY**
Until Sun 28 June
Norwich Arts Centre
An exhibition of contemporary jewellery represents four makers using a variety of materials, from pewter and textiles to silver and rosewood. And a variety of ideas, from witty articulated brooches to designs inspired by leaves and wrought iron work.

(g)

□ **JULIAN JOSEPH**
Wed 6 May, 8pm
Norwich Arts Centre
One of the finest young jazz pianists in the world, Julian Joseph began with Courtney Pine's first quartet and recently produced a 'startling debut album of superb musicianship' with Jean Toussaint (saxes), Alec Dankworth (bass) and Mark Mondesir (drums).

(h)

□ **LUNCHTIME CONCERT**
Thurs 14 May, 1 pm
The King of Hearts
Sarah Higgins (flute) and Maureen Smith (piano) perform works by Handel and Prokoviev.

(i)

□ **MADDY PRIOR AND RICK KEMP**
Sat 2 May, 8pm
Norwich Arts Centre
Central to Britain's folk scene, both as husband-and-wife and individual performers. Rick is renowned for bass-guitar and Maddy still sings for Steeleye Span with her 'crystal voice and brilliant harmonies.'

(j)

□ **WHEN THE BOATS CAME IN**
Fri 22 May, 8pm
Angles Centre
A kaleidoscopic picture of the great East Anglian herring fishery and a musical tribute to the men and women who lived their lives through it.

(k)

□ **MY MOTHER SAID I NEVER SHOULD**
Sat 30 May, 7.30pm
Angles Centre
First national tour of this play about the way the private relationship between mother and daughter is put under pressure by each generations public goal for the 'ideal' woman; home-baking wife to earth mother to tough executive.

(l)

□ **AN AMERICAN TAIL (U)**
Sat 2 May, 2.30pm
Cinema City
Delightful Steven Spielberg-produced animated film about the adventures of a family of Russian mice who emigrated to America in the 1890s.

(m)

□ **RETURN JOURNEY**
Sat 9 May, 8pm
Norwich Arts Centre
With sell-out shows around the world and audiences clamouring for more, Norwich Arts Centre brings back Bob Kingdom with Dylan Thomas, for his haunting re-creation of the poet's own live recitals.

(n)

□ **TRIO SONNERIE**
Sun 10 May, 7.30pm
The King of Hearts
A portrait of love and other musical pictures, with works by Marais, Clerambault and Couperin. Monica Hugget (violin), Sarah Cunningham (viola da gamba), and Mitzi Myerson (harpsichord) with Nancy Argenta (soprano).

(o)

□ **ODDSOCKS THEATRE COMPANY**
Sun 24 May, 1pm and 3pm
Raveningham Hall Gardens
The eighteenth century hall of Raveningham, with its fine gardens, makes an impressive backdrop to this show, specifically designed for families with children. Take a picnic and make a day of it.

(p)

❻ Scan the entertainment listings to find the following information:

1 Which concert will not cost you anything?
2 How many artists are showing their work in June?
3 Which performers are married?
4 Which musician has recently made a record?
5 What are the two open-air entertainments?
6 Which play is being performed all over the country?
7 What is the connection between James Dodds and The Angles Centre?
8 Where can you see a cartoon film?
9 Which event takes place every year?
10 Which two events have connections with poetry?

❼ Look back through the listings and underline all the positive words and phrases which are used to attract the reader. Make a list of those which are superlatives, e.g. *one of the fin<u>est</u>*.

❽ Listen to the introduction to a radio arts review programme and complete the information in the left-hand column of the chart opposite.

❾ Listen to the critics talking about the film, the play and the exhibition and make notes on the chart of words and phrases used to give positive and negative opinions.

	Positive	Negative
'Howards End' (PG) _____		
'The Taming of the Shrew' _____		
_____		
The Royal Academy, Piccadilly		

VOCABULARY

❶ Working in pairs, discuss the following:

1. Do you often use a dictionary?
2. What kind of dictionary do you use – bilingual or monolingual?
3. Rank the following uses in order of importance to you:
   - to find out about word meanings
   - to check spellings
   - to check stress and pronunciation
   - to do some grammar work
   - to find out about the history of the word
   - to help with translations

Compare your list with your partner's.

❷ Look at these dictionary entries. Draw lines from the boxes to connect with the relevant part of the dictionary entries. The first one has been done for you.

> This is the headword. It is the word that you are looking up in the dictionary.

> This is the phonetic transcription. It tells you how to say the word.

> This is the definition. It explains the meaning of the word.

> This abbreviation tells you something about the grammar of the word. It explains whether it is a verb, adjective, adverb, noun, etc.

> This shows you how the headword can combine with other words.

> This shows how new words can be made from the headword.

> This is an example sentence. It shows how the word is used.

pur-chase [pə́:tʃəs] *vt.* (P 1) ❶ buy ; get in exchange for money. ❷ (fig.) get by effort, struggle, or sacrifice, as *a dearly purchased victory* (i.e. in a battle in which many men are killed). ❸ (on a ship) raise an anchor, etc., by means of a pulley, lever, etc. —*n.* ❶ Ⓤ the act of buying ; getting something in exchange for money. ❷ Ⓒ a thing which is purchased. *He filled the car with his purchases.* ❸ Ⓤ value; worth; esp. as reckoned in the annual yield of a house, etc., as *thirty years' purchase* (i.e. thirty times the annual rent). *His life is not worth a day's purchase* (fig., he is near death). ❹ (sing.) a firm hold or grip to help one to move something ; leverage. ❺ (fig.) an advantage or influence ; a means of increasing an advantage. **pur-chas-er** [pə́:tʃəsə] *n.* a buyer.

> This is the headword. It is the word that you are looking up in the dictionary.

> This is the phonetic transcription. It tells you how to say the word.

> This is the definition. It explains the meaning of the word.

> This abbreviation tells you something about the grammar of the word. It explains whether it is a verb, adjective, adverb, noun, etc.

> This shows you how the headword can combine with other words.

in-vis-i-ble [invízibl] *adj.* that cannot be seen. *Many stars are invisible without a telescope.* **invisible exports [imports],** money that goes out of [comes into] a country, as interest on capital, payments for shipping services, insurance, tourist expenditure, etc. that account for the apparent difference between a country's imports and exports. **invisible ink,** ink which, when used for writing, can be seen only when it is heated. **in-vis-i-bil-i-ty** [invìzibíliti] *n.* **in-vis-i-bly,** *adv.*

> This shows how new words can be made from the headword.

> This is an example sentence. It shows how the word is used.

> This is the headword. It is the word that you are looking up in the dictionary.

> This is the phonetic transcription. It tells you how to say the word.

> This is the definition. It explains the meaning of the word.

> This abbreviation tells you something about the grammar of the word. It explains whether it is a verb, adjective, adverb, noun, etc.

> This shows you how the headword can combine with other words.

> This shows how new words can be made from the headword.

> This is an example sentence. It shows how the word is used.

tongue [tʌŋ] *n.* ❶ the movable organ in the mouth, used for licking, in tasting, and in talking. **give tongue,** (of people) shout or speak loudly ; (of dogs) bark. **have one's tongue in one's cheek,** speak ironically ; say something one does not really mean. **have lost one's tongue,** be too shy to speak. **find one's tongue,** begin to speak after a period of silence due to shyness. **tongue=tied,** *adj.* silent ; unable to speak through shyness, fear, etc. **hold one's tongue,** be silent. ❷ a language, as *one's mother tongue* ; *the gift of tongues* (i.e. ability to speak foreign languages). ❸ a way of speaking. *He has a ready tongue* (i.e. speaks easily ; answers promptly and well). *Keep a civil tongue in your head* (i.e. don't be rude) ! ❹ Ⓒ & Ⓤ the tongue of an animal as food. ❺ anything resembling a tongue, as *the tongue of a boot* (i.e. the strip of leather under the laces) ; *the tongue of a bell* (i.e. the hammer that strikes the sides) ; *tongues of flame* (i.e. long, thin flames). **=tongued** [tʌŋd] *adj.* having a particular kind of tongue, voice, sound, etc., as *a silver-tongued orator.*

❸ Look at the text *Festival Break*.

1. What do you think it is about?
2. Who do you think it is written for?
3. Who do you think wrote it?
4. Where do you think you would find it?

WHY NOT TAKE A SPECIAL
Festival Break

Brighton's Tourism and Resort department and Brighton Festival have combined to offer a unique opportunity to visit Festival events and sample the delights of Britain's premier resort.

Brighton boasts the fabulous Royal Pavilion, the famous seaside palace of the Prince Regent, splendid Victorian churches, antiquarian bookshops, boutiques, specialist galleries, markets and antique shops. There is fine architecture to be explored, as well as all the fun of a seaside town.

Long the home of performers, craftsmen and writers, Brighton is renowned for its artistic tradition. A colourful and cosmopolitan centre, the town offers a selection of pubs, restaurants and bistros for every taste and purse.

The picturesque towns and villages in the Sussex countryside, houses of historic interest and the South Downs are also in very easy reach.

Brighton Festival packs more than four hundred events into a little over three weeks in May. What better time and place can there be to take a lively break?

Festival Holiday Breaks enable you to take advantage of special accommodation rates and secure your tickets for all the shows and events you want to see during the Brighton Festival.

To book, select your events and hotel, fill in the form overleaf, and send it to us. We'll do the rest.

❹ Read the passage more closely. Underline all the words that have positive associations, e.g. *unique opportunity*.

❺ Find the word or expression in the passage that means the same as:

short holiday, number one, easily accessible, pleasures, special chance, international, outstanding, prices, joined together

❻ Working in pairs, use your dictionaries to study the following words:

delights, boasts, renowned, packs, selection, secure

- What type of word is it?
- What form is it in? (singular/plural, present tense, etc.)
- What does the word mean as it is used in the passage?
- What else can the word mean?
- How do you say it?
- What other words can be made from it?
- What other words do you link with it?

❼ Find the odd one out in the following sets. What are your reasons?

- *shop, boutique, gallery, market, stall*
- *pocket, purse, wallet, money-belt, change*
- *fabulous, weird, excellent, brilliant, splendid*
- *church, synagogue, mosque, hall, temple*

❽ Using your dictionary, group the following words under these headings.

PERFORMER	CRAFTSMAN	WRITER

journalist, carpenter, potter, soloist, star, scribe, editor, mason, diva, blacksmith, clerk, actor, ballerina, poet, printer, tightrope-walker

❾ Complete the sentences using words made by changing the form of the key word.

compete

His dream was to take part in an international _____ .
To be at the top of your sport you must be really _____ .
At the Olympics, _____ come to take part from all over the world.

athlete

Gymnastics is her favourite event but she also competes in _____ .
Even as a baby crawling on the floor, she was _____ , flexible and fast.

mountain

As a sport, I love _____ .
This part of England is not particularly _____ .

cycle

_____ is a great sport.
Yes, I suppose I would class myself as a serious amateur _____ .

❿ Consider these questions and answer them for the sports in the table below.

- Is it played on a court, a course or a pitch?
- Can you add *-er* to the name of the game or do you have to say e.g. *a (netball) player*?
- Is the score measured in points or goals?
- Who makes the decisions and enforces the rules, a referee or an umpire?
- What is it played with (rackets/balls/bats etc.)?

	FOOTBALL	TENNIS	CRICKET	BASKETBALL
Played on a				
Players				
Score				
Decisions made by				
Played with				

⓫ Working in groups, think of other common sports and use the same questions to work at the vocabulary of the sport.

⓬ What can happen in these places? List the activities.

stadium, gallery, ground, auditorium, court, hall, pitch, alley

⓭ Imagine that you are speaking to someone whose English is not as good as yours. How would you explain the following? Use a dictionary to help you if you are stuck.

amateur, league, professional, games, side, team, points, supporter, fan, match, opponent, rival

PROJECT – A 'WHAT'S ON' GUIDE

Your class is going to produce a guide to the entertainments and activities in the town (or area of the city) where you are studying. There may already be a locally-produced 'What's On' guide or section of your local newspaper, but your project should produce a guide *for this week only* which is specially designed for other students in your school.

STAGE ONE: Preparation and research

Before you start to design and write your Guide, you will need to find out what different kinds of entertainment and activities are available – and what your readers are most interested in. Remember that the Guide is for other students. It should include information about everything that is happening in your town, but there should be more space for those things which are likely to be most popular.

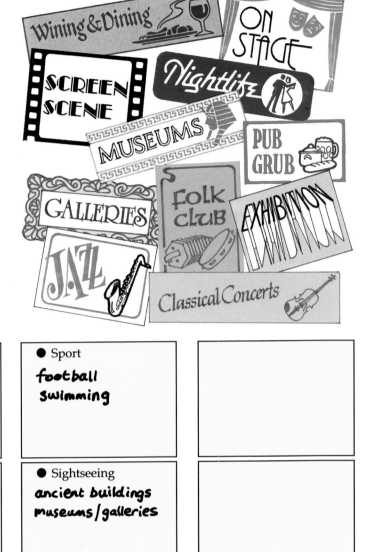

❶ In small groups, brainstorm as many different types of entertainment and activities as you can. Below are some general headings with one or two examples under each heading to help you. Can you think of any other headings?

● Cultural events	● Eating out	● Sport	
theatre *classical music*	*restaurants* *fast food*	*football* *swimming*	
● Nightlife	● Clubs	● Sightseeing	
discos *nightclubs*	*keep fit* *aerobics*	*ancient buildings* *museums / galleries*	

Exchange your ideas with other groups. Which examples were the same? Which were different?

❷ Prepare a simple survey questionnaire to find out which entertainments/activities are most popular among students in your school. What will be the best way to design your questionnaire? Below are some examples – though you may have your own ideas.

● **Simple response**

Example: Which of the following places have you visited in the last two weeks?

cinema ❑
disco ❑
swimming pool ❑

● **Response + frequency**

Example: How many times have you visited the places listed below since you arrived in Britain?

	never	once	twice	three times or more
theatre museum health club				

● **Ranking**

Example: Mark the following entertainments/activities in the order of your preference (1 = most popular).

classical concerts ❑ eating out ❑ jazz clubs ❑

Remember to include some 'open' questions to give your interviewees the chance to add their own ideas.

Example: Are there any other places which you enjoy visiting in your free time?
What do you think about _____?

❸ Collect information, news and reviews about entertainment and leisure activities in your area. Where can you get the information? Here are some possibilities – though again you may have your own ideas.

- local 'What's On' magazine
- local newspaper (or local free paper)
- tourist office information
- posters in the streets
- computer database in the local library
- school noticeboards
- information from teachers, host families, other students

Think about the best way of collecting the information. Different groups could be responsible either for different kinds of leisure activities (e.g. one group finding out about cinemas) or for different sources of information (e.g. one group visiting the tourist office).

When you are collecting information (newspaper cuttings, leaflets, your own notes), make sure you have all the practical details that your readers will want to know, e.g. addresses, telephone numbers, opening hours, prices, etc.

STAGE TWO: Planning and editing

The next step is to organise all the information that you have collected and to think about the most appropriate way to present it to your readers. You might arrange the Guide with one section showing events which are on throughout the week and separate sections for things happening on particular days. Or there could be a section for each different kind of leisure activity (e.g. cinema, sport, music).

Use the following ideas to help you plan and write your Guide.

1 Where? When? How much?

- Location. Is everyone likely to know the place or do you need to give details of how to get there?

- Times. Is the event/activity available every day of the week? What are the opening hours/time(s) of performances etc? Are times different e.g. on Sundays?

- Prices. Is the event free or do you have to pay? Are tickets all at one price or is there a range of prices? Are there any discounts or special offers for students? Do restaurant prices include drinks?

- Booking. Is it necessary to reserve tickets in advance? If so, can they be booked by telephone or do you have to go to the box office in person? Can advance tickets be bought anywhere else?

2 Reviews and Previews

- Ask someone in your group (or in another group) to write a short review of any of the entertainments/ leisure activities you are including in your listings. These mini-reviews should only be five or six lines long, giving essential information about the place/event and your personal opinion of it. (Some of the vocabulary from the listening task in Section 5 may be helpful here.)

- Try to get some information for a preview, like those in Section 5 on pages 26-7. Give your readers the most important details and say who you think will find the place/event interesting and enjoyable.

3 Editorial Tasks

An Editorial Board should be responsible for the planning and organisation of the whole Guide.

a Work out how much time the class will need to complete the project and give deadlines to groups for handing you their sections of the Guide.

b Send editorial assistants to each of the other groups to give advice and suggestions.

c Make sure that groups are not producing any of the same information.

d Act as messengers between groups to help with the collection of reviews and further information.

e Write a short introduction to the Guide. Explain how it is organised and how readers can find different kinds of information.

STAGE THREE: Presentation

You should now think about the best way to present your 'What's On' Guide, so that other students can use it.

- Format. Magazine or wall display? Is it possible to provide individual copies of the Guide for all the students in your school or will you make one copy for each classroom? Is there a place in the school where a wall display would be seen by everyone?

- Layout. How could the page design of the Guide help other students to find the information they are looking for quickly and easily? Will the pages be easier to read if you use one column or two? How can you emphasise headings (e.g. underlining, capital letters)? Can you design symbols for different sections of the Guide?

- Style. Have you used the same style throughout the Guide? E.g., decide whether you want to use 8 pm, 8.00 or 20.00. If you have used abbreviations, will they be understood by everyone, or do you need a key? E.g. 'Tel.' for 'telephone' will be familiar to most people, but 'perf.' for 'performance' may need to be explained.

- Illustrations. Have you got any photographs (either your own or examples from newspapers and magazines) which will make the guide more attractive and interesting to look at?

REVIEW

PROJECT EVALUATION

Was your project successful? Use the questions below to discuss the various stages of production, as well as the Guide itself.

Preparation and research

How easy was it to brainstorm all the different kinds of leisure activities to include in the Guide? Did you think of them all immediately or did you remember some later on? How successful was your questionnaire? Did the questions you asked produce the right kind of information about the popularity of different activities? Where did you go to get the information you needed? Did you find out everything you wanted to know?

Planning and editing

Did you decide to present the information you had collected as a daily programme or by different kinds of activities? What were the advantages/disadvantages of the method you chose? How useful were the suggestions given about information to include in the Guide? Is there anything you would add? What do you think of the reviews and previews which were written for the Guide? Which ones were most informative? How well did the editors do their jobs? Could they have been more helpful in any way?

Presentation

Are you satisfied with the results of your project? Have you had a positive response from other students? Do you think the Guide is attractive and easy to use? Are there any improvements which could be made to it?

THINKING ABOUT LANGUAGE LEARNING

MAKING THE MOST OF YOUR STAY IN BRITAIN

❶ Divide the class into two sets (A and B). Each set should then split up into smaller groups to consider the following questions.

A groups

What opportunities do you have while you are staying in Britain to read and to listen to English? Think about all the different written and spoken 'texts' that you see and hear every day outside the classroom. Here are some examples. How many more can you add to each list?

Written

newspapers
notices
advertisements

Spoken

songs
other people's conversations
TV programmes

B groups

What opportunities do you have while you are staying in Britain to speak and to write in English? Think about all the different situations when you use the language outside the classroom. Here are some examples. How many more can you add to each list?

Speaking

using the phone
chatting to other students
making enquiries

Writing

filling in forms
noting appointments
writing down song lyrics

❷ Form new groups with equal numbers from A and B groups. Exchange your lists and see if the new group members can add any ideas.

❸ Have you had any communication problems since you arrived in Britain? Think of situations when you have misunderstood someone or when other people have misunderstood you. Share your experiences and choose two or three of the funniest (or the most embarrassing!) examples to tell the rest of the class.

❹ Imagine that a friend is coming to Britain to study English on a short course like yours. Your friend wants to know how to improve his/her English outside the classroom. Using ideas from the lists that you have made, decide on ten pieces of advice that you would give. When you have agreed on ten items, write them on a poster to display on the wall of the classroom.

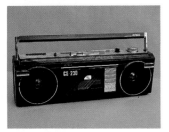

❺ Working in pairs, make a list of all the different situations in which you need to understand spoken English.

❻ What makes listening to English easier or more difficult? Tick (✓) any of the following statements you agree with.

- Strange accents become easier to understand as you get used to them. ❑
- I can follow much faster speech than I could when I started learning English. ❑
- I still find it difficult to follow a conversation when there are more than two speakers, especially if they talk at the same time. ❑
- It's easier to follow what people are saying on TV or at the cinema than on the radio or on the telephone. ❑
- If I know something about the topic, listening is usually much easier. ❑
- I sometimes get lost when the topic changes. ❑
- I find that listening is easier when I'm not too tired. ❑

❼ Choose three of the situations which you listed in Exercise 1 above and discuss the following questions.

1   Why are you listening (e.g. for general interest, for particular bits of information, for pleasure etc.)?

2   What kinds of words and phrases do you expect to hear?

3   Do you need to understand every word or just the general meaning/a few key words?

4   Does the speaker give you any signals which will help you to follow the message (e.g. announcing the topic, telling the listener what points s/he is going to talk about, repeating the main ideas etc.)?

5   How easy is it to predict what is going to be said?

❽ How can you improve your listening comprehension? Discuss the following suggestions and add your own ideas.

- Use songs and stories with accompanying texts. Many cassettes and CDs have song lyrics printed on the cover and you will find plenty of 'talking books' in bookshops and record shops. Practise listening with and without the printed texts.

- Use newspapers with radio and TV news. Take two or three main news stories and make notes of the main points in each one. Then listen to the news on radio (or TV) to see if the same points are mentioned.

- Listen to one of the recordings from this book and note down a maximum of ten key words. Use the words you have written down to reconstruct as much as you can of the original recording.

- Listen in on other people's conversations and make notes of words and phrases you hear. Use your notes to begin lists of vocabulary items which you can expect to hear in particular situations.

WRITING

❾ Look back over your experience of living and learning in Britain during the last two weeks. Think about your accommodation, the people you have met, the places you have visited and all the things you have seen and heard. Write a letter to your English teacher at home, telling him/her about:

- things which are just as you expected
- things which have surprised you
- how you have been spending your free time
- how you have been practising and improving your English outside the classroom.

Summarise your ideas in note form and plan the presentation of your letter before you write it.

REVIEW

Think about the work you have done in this unit and continue the learner diary which you began at the end of Unit 1. Use the following headings to organise your diary entry.

- Topics - new information
- New language - grammar and vocabulary
- Language practice - reading and listening/speaking and writing
- Accuracy - *I feel more confident about ... /I'm not so sure about ...*
- Fluency - *I'm getting better at ... /I still find it difficult to ...*
- Summary - *At the moment I feel ...*

❶ The pictures below illustrate different kinds of music which are popular with British audiences. How many do you recognise? Where do you think the performers come from? What kinds of people go to hear them?

a

b

c

d

e

f

g

h

i

j

❷ Match each of the pictures with one of the following:

| disco | rock | orchestral music |

| opera | chamber music | jazz |

| heavy metal | folk | blues |

| country and western |

❸ Which of the types of music pictured in exercise 1 can you hear on the tape? Write the names in the spaces below.

Extract

A _____

B _____

C _____

D _____

E _____

F _____

❹ Did you like/dislike the extracts you have heard? Put them in order from the one you liked the most (1) to the one you liked the least (6).

❺ Compare your choice with a partner and find out more about each other's musical tastes. Ask about:

- favourite kind(s) of music
- particular dislikes
- going to concerts
- favourite performer(s)
- CD/tape collection
- playing an instrument

LIKES AND DISLIKES

6 Before you listen, discuss the following questions with your partner:

1 When do you enjoy listening to music?
  a while you are working
  b while you are doing something else (e.g. driving, having a bath, cooking)
  c in the morning as soon as you get up
  d in the evening when you are relaxing

2 How do you prefer to listen?
  a at a live concert
  b on a good quality sound system
  c on a personal stereo
  d on video

3 Do you always listen to the same kind of music?

7 Now listen to three people talking about a new British radio station. While you listen, make notes about their likes and dislikes on the chart below:

	likes	dislikes	phrases used
Speaker 1			
Speaker 2			
Speaker 3			

8 Listen again and write down the phrases used by the three speakers to express their likes and dislikes.

9 These people have all been to the same concert, but feel very differently about it. Their opinions have been mixed up. Can you match pairs of sentences, so that what they are saying makes more sense? Then, number the speech bubbles from 1 (strongest like) to 6 (strongest dislike).

I LOVED IT. IT WAS TERRIBLE.

I DIDN'T ENJOY IT AT ALL. IT WAS ALL RIGHT.

I LOATHED IT. IT WAS ABSOLUTELY BRILLIANT.

I THOROUGHLY ENJOYED IT. IT WASN'T VERY GOOD.

I QUITE LIKED IT. IT WAS PRETTY BORING.

I DIDN'T LIKE IT VERY MUCH. IT WAS VERY GOOD INDEED.

'THE YOUTH OF TODAY'

❶ Look at the people here. They each represent certain youth groups and cultures. For each one, write down all the words that you associate with the person(s) in the picture.

a

'Mods' = modern. 1960s.
Popular group – 'The Who'.
Scooters. Clean and
smartly dressed.

b

c

d

e

f

❷ Work in pairs. Share your notes and list the youth groups and cultures that you have noticed while you have been in Britain. How is this similar or different from the fashions in your country? Has a particular youth culture influenced you? How?

READING

❸ Read the poem below and write a title for it.

> He was
> A wild young man
> He couldn't care
> For what they thought, or said –
> He had his own ideas.
> his looks provoked his father to protest:
> 'In my young days
> A man who dressed like *that*
> Was not a man.'
> his mother grew afraid
> Of this fierce strange young man
> – Her son.
>
> He's alright now
> He has 'improved' with age
> 'I knew it – just a passing phase
> They all go through,'
> His mother smiles.
> He's got a good, safe job,
> A wife, a lawn-mower ...
> He's alright now.
>
> *Lesley Rigg*

❹ 1 Imagine that you are the young man's father. How would you speak his words in the poem? What feelings are you trying to express?

  2 Imagine that you are the young man's mother. How would you speak her words in the poem? What feelings are you trying to express?

  3 Add five more items to continue the list: *A wife, a lawn-mower ...*

❺ **Role-play.** Working in groups of three or four choose one of the following character roles: the mother; the father; the wild young man/woman; the wild young man/woman's friend.

  The situation. There is a family wedding. The father's youngest brother is getting married. The wild young man/woman doesn't really want to go to the wedding because there is an important concert in another town on the same day. The wild young man/woman agrees to go to the wedding on condition that s/he can bring a friend and then leave early in order to get to the concert. S/he does not want to wear formal clothes.

  Task. Stay in the role that you have chosen and discuss the situation.

WHAT DO YOU THINK?

❻ Read the following statements about youth in Britain and decide whether you agree or disagree. Compare Britain with the situation in your own country and say what the family, government, police etc. could/should do or are doing.

  1 It is dangerous to walk around on your own at night because there are so many youth gangs waiting to rob people or get into fights.

  2 There are plenty of things for young people to do in Britain.

  3 The most dangerous thing facing young people in Britain today is drugs.

  4 Young people in Britain are too busy earning money to be bothered with radical youth cultures any more. They don't care about politics.

  5 Young people in Britain are far more sensitive and care more about the environment than the generations before them. They do not want to be different, they want to protect what they have.

SECTION 3

READING

Before you read

a

b

❶ Study the pictures in **a** and **b** and write down two lists of all the words that you think of.

❷ Working in pairs, compare your lists. What words have you both chosen? Add to your lists.

❸ Take your partner's lists and then draw lines between words and around groups of words to show how they can be linked. You can link the words in any way you like.

While you read

❹ Underline all of the words in the poem that you link with the rich people and put a ring around all of the words that you link with the poor people.

❺ Write down any questions that you have about the poem.

Interruption at the Opera House

At the very beginning of an important symphony,
while the rich and famous were settling into their
                 quietly expensive boxes,
a man came crashing through the crowds,
carrying in his hand a cage in which
the rightful owner of the music sat,
yellow and tiny and very poor;
and taking onto the rostrum this rather timid bird
he turned up the microphones, and it sang.

'A very original beginning to the evening,' said the
                 crowds,
quietly glancing at their programmes to find
the significance of the intrusion.

Meanwhile at the box office the organizers of the evening
were arranging for small and uniformed attendants
to evict, even forcefully, the intruders.
But as the attendants, poor and gathered from the
                 nearby slums at little expense,
went rushing down the aisles to do their job
they heard, above the coughing and the irritable rattling
                 of jewels,
a sound that filled their heads with light,
and from somewhere inside them there bubbled up a
                 stream,
and there came a breeze on which their youth was
                 carried.
How sweetly the bird sang!

And though soon the fur-wrapped crowds
were leaving their boxes and in confusion were winding
                                    their way home

still the attendants sat in the aisles,
and some, so delighted at what they heard, rushed out
                                          to call

their families and friends.

And their children came,
sleepy for it was late in the evening,
very late in the evening,
and they hardly knew if they had done with dreaming
or had begun again.

In all the tenement blocks
the lights were clicking on,
and the rightful owner of the music,
tiny but no longer timid sang
for the rightful owners of the song.

Brian Patten

After you have read the poem

❻ Work in pairs and share your questions.

❼ Imagine that you have been given the task of making a
film from the poem.
    Choose what you think are the most important images
and events in the poem and using the format below,
draw the film director's storyboard and add her/his
notes for each shot. When you have finished, display
your storyboards and discuss the differences.

SOUNDS OF THE ORCHESTRA TUNING UP. STRONG COLOURS – REDS, GOLDS – DIAMONDS OR PEARLS ROUND THE WOMEN'S NECKS.

WRITING

❽ The class should divide into two groups, **A** and **B**.

Group A

Imagine that you were at the Opera House on the night
of the interruption. Working alone, in pairs or in small
groups, write a dialogue that retells the events of the
evening as you explain what happened to a friend. You
should try to explain your feelings and show what you
think should be done.

Group B

Imagine that you were someone from the slums who
came to the Opera House on the evening when the bird
sang out to its new audience. Working alone, in pairs or
in small groups, write a dialogue that retells the events
of the evening as you explain what happened to a
friend. You should try to explain your feelings and show
what you believe.

SECTION 4

LANGUAGE PRACTICE

CONDITIONAL SENTENCES

❶ Match the sentences on the left with the comments on the right.

If we book the tickets in advance, they will be cheaper.	It's possible, but we probably won't do it.
If we bought the tickets at the concert, they would be more expensive.	It's impossible because things happened differently.
If I left home, I would find a flat in London.	It's only a dream.
If I was a rock star, I'd buy my own recording studio.	It's possible and we will probably do it.
If I'd been to university, I would have got a better job.	It's possible, but rather unlikely.

❷ Read the following sentences and answer the questions with *Yes, No* or *Don't know.*

1 If Robert works hard, he'll pass the exam.

   ● Is Robert going to work hard?
   ● Will he pass the exam?

2 If Kate was more organised, she wouldn't lose things.

   ● Is Kate organised?
   ● Does she lose things?

3 If his parents hadn't been so busy, they could have helped him.

   ● Were his parents busy?
   ● Did they help him?

4 Steve might get a job if he didn't wear an ear-ring.

   ● Does Steve wear an ear-ring?
   ● Will he get a job?

5 Jane wouldn't have met Chris if she hadn't gone to the party.

   ● Did Jane go to the party?
   ● Did she meet Chris?

6 We won't be able to see the stage unless we get good seats.

   ● Have we got good seats?
   ● Will we be able to see the stage?

❸ Look carefully at the following sentences and say who you think is speaking, who they are speaking to and what the situation is.

1 If you go straight ahead, you'll see the cinema on your left.
2 If I know the answer, I'll tell you.
3 If I knew the answer, I'd tell you.
4 If he had taken my advice, he would have got home safely.
5 He'd be much healthier if he didn't smoke so much.
6 If you need help, you only have to ask.
7 If you'll give me a moment, I'll try to find the information.
8 If you wanted a lift, why didn't you ask me?
9 I'd catch an earlier train if I were you.
10 You wouldn't have got lost if you'd followed my directions.

Use the sentences above to decide whether or not you agree with the following statements.

a There are three main types of conditional sentence.
b There are only three types of conditional sentence.
c The choice of tense forms depends on how probable or likely the situation seems to the speaker.
d Conditional sentences always begin with *if*.
e The *if* clause is always separated from the main clause by a comma.
f *If* is never followed by *will*.
g *Would* and *had* both have the same short form.
h Either clause of a conditional sentence can be negative.

❹ Sort the sentences below into three groups of situations or events under the following headings. Three examples have been done for you.

a possible or likely, now or in the future

b impossible or possible, but very unlikely now or in the future

c impossible now because of something that did/did not happen in the past

1 If my parents had given me more freedom, I would not have left home. *c*

2 Supposing you went to the States, what would you want to see?

3 You can borrow my CD player as long as you promise to take care of it.

4 If I had five hundred pounds, I would buy a new sound system. *b*

5 Without the example of the Beatles, today's pop music would have been very different.

6 Unless it rains, I'll go to the rock festival at the weekend.

7 If we leave early, we'll get there in time. *a*

8 Had I known how far it was, I wouldn't have walked.

9 If only I lived in a big city, I'd have a more interesting life.

10 I'll invite Jane to the party provided she doesn't bring Peter.

11 If I'd seen the label, I would have realised it was more expensive.

12 Assuming money wasn't a problem, what kind of car would you want?

❺ Match the following meanings with the conditional sentences below.

advice   condition   offer   prediction   promise
regret   request   warning   threat   wish

1 If I'd realised that repairs were so expensive, I would have bought a cheaper model.

2 If only I could play the guitar!

3 If it's raining, I'll lend you an umbrella.

4 If you lend me £10, I'll pay you back tomorrow.

5 If you say that again, you'll be sorry!

6 You'll have an accident if you're not careful!

7 They won't let you into the disco unless you're wearing a tie.

8 If you'll wait a moment, I'll see if the manager is free.

9 If I were in your shoes, I'd look for another job.

10 If you don't turn the music down, I'll call the police!

❻ Complete the following dialogue with the correct forms of the verbs:

Father: It's half past twelve. Why are you so late?

Son: If I told you, you (*not believe*) me.

Father: You missed the bus again, I suppose. If you (*be*) late again, I won't let you go to any more rock concerts. Why didn't you phone?

Son: Dad, if I (*stop*) to phone, I would have missed the last bus. What was I supposed to do?

Father: You should have phoned. I (*pay*) for a taxi if you miss the bus next time. Your mother and I were getting quite worried.

Son: I'm sorry. If I (*know*) you'd pay for a taxi, I'd have been home half an hour ago.

❼ The sentences in this exercise are the lyrics of *If*, a song by the rock group, Pink Floyd. The main clauses on the right have been mixed up. Can you match them with the *if* clauses on the left?

If I were a swan	I'd be late
If I were a train	I could hide
If I were a good man	I could bend
If I were asleep	please don't put your wires in my brain
If I were afraid	I'd talk with you more often than I do
If I go insane	I'd be late again
If I were the moon	will you still let me join in with the game?
If I were a bow	I'd be cool
If I were a good man	I'd be gone
If I were alone	I could dream
If I were with you	I'd understand the spaces between friends
If I go insane	I'd be home and dry
If I were a train	I would cry

❽ Complete the following sentences about yourself:

1 If I come back next year, _____

_____

2 _____

if I had enough money.

3 If I had understood more English, _____

_____

4 _____

if I hadn't come to Britain.

5 If I were British, _____

_____

6 _____

if I can.

SECTION 5

❶ What connections can you make among the words and phrases set out below? Draw lines between those which you think can be linked in some way.

banking   teenagers

career   industry

rock music   making a living

education   training

steady job   qualifications

business   respectability

diploma   market

❷ Compare your ideas with a partner and explain the connections you have made.

READING

❸ Read the text below and answer the following questions.

1 What would you say is the purpose of the text?
2 Who do you think the writer is?
3 What kind of readership is it intended to appeal to?
4 Where and when do you think it was published?

Rock music and education

They said it would never last, but here we are almost four decades later, with rock and roll bigger – and some would say better – than ever.

Foreign earnings from the music business are second only to insurance and banking, which will give you some idea of the size and scale of the market.

In those heady, far-off days of the 1950s, rock music was something your mother disliked and your father tried to ignore.

10 For most teenagers of that time, school was followed by a steady job. Girls inevitably found themselves in 'respectable' jobs and then got married! For lads it meant an apprenticeship of some sort. Getting a trade under your belt was the order of the day. In retrospect this was a short-sighted view, as most of the people who became tradesmen/women are having to retrain for something else, following the virtual demise of industry in Britain.

Some fortunate or unfortunate teenagers (depending on your point of view) managed to go to college or university 20 to study some sort of 'ology'.

Before the end of the 50s, the TV networks were catering for the demands of youth and rock and roll. This took the form of programmes such as *Oh Boy!* and *Six-Five Special*, which were the forerunners of the 1960s' *Ready, Steady, Go!* and the more sanitised *Top of the Pops*.

Schools covered all the traditionally relevant subjects, including the 3 Rs, which may have included music, but definitely did not include rock and roll.

School has regularly received acknowledgement in pop 30 songs. Chuck Berry, Rod Stewart, Alice Cooper and Pink Floyd were some of the artists who used the word and sometimes the imagery associated with an experience everyone goes through, or in some cases, endures.

Since 1955, pop/rock music has gradually become more acceptable to the Establishment. Indeed some pop/rock acts have come perilously close to becoming the Establishment themselves – the Beatles with their MBEs and Elton John and Mick Jagger, who seem to have a foot in the door of Buckingham Palace.

40 The 1960s witnessed a redrawing of cultural boundaries, with the music business in particular at the cutting edge.

In line with this generally wider acceptance and understanding that this form of music would not disappear overnight, schools and colleges have in the last few years begun to offer courses and facilities that can enhance and complement interest in pop/rock music.

In comprehensive schools across the country, under the auspices of Local Education Authorities, it has been realised that interest in music and other culturally related 50 areas can be developed and encouraged by providing instruments and equipment of the type normally seen at rock concerts.

For those who at 16+ wish to follow up an interest in the music business as performers, technicians or administrators and gain some nationally recognised qualifications, many colleges offer BTEC National Diploma courses in Performing Arts.

Not all of these deal specifically with the music industry. However, there are at least two colleges offering courses 60 specifically centred on the business and the performing/recording of pop music.

Of course, there is not any direct qualification or route of success, but that is true of other careers as well. The whole point of completing a college course dealing with what is, after all, a precarious way to make a living is that it can give interested people an opportunity to experiment and develop their particular talent within a creative environment, whilst gaining some of the skills that may give them the necessary edge when opportunity strikes.

70 Neath College in South Wales, which pioneered the first National Diploma specialising in rock music, is about to

launch a new Higher National Diploma in Performing Arts. This will offer a course of study of the music business at almost degree level. The course has been devised following close consultation with various people within the industry and it is planned to offer students periods of work experience at intervals during the two years of the course.

80 The trend within the vocational sector of education for the 16+ age group is increasingly to provide courses that are interesting for students and relevant to jobs and careers. The dust-laden corridors of academia are gradually being stirred up by Marshall stacks and assorted sequencers.

The future looks bright for budding rock musicians who wish to acquire formal qualifications. We may well see a Ph.D. in Rock Music in the future.

It may only be rock and roll to you, but increasingly it's homework to someone else.

❹ Find words or phrases in the text which have the following meanings:

1 periods of ten years
2 initial period of training in a first job
3 looking back
4 near-collapse
5 academic (usually scientific) subject of study [slang]
6 supplying what is wanted
7 cleaned up so as to look respectable
8 basic school subjects (reading, writing and arithmetic)
9 suffers (or puts up with)
10 dangerously
11 uncertain and risky
12 the area of education concerned with job-related skills

❺ Look carefully at how the following idioms are used in the text. Decide whether the definitions given are true or false and correct the ones that you think are false.

1 *getting something under your belt:* acquiring some kind of experience (lines 13-14)
2 *the order of the day:* something unusual or exceptional (line 14)
3 *the Establishment:* the people and institutions who have power in public life (line 35)
4 *to have a foot in the door:* to be unacceptable in somebody's house (lines 38-9)
5 *to be at the cutting edge:* to be a leading influence in new developments (line 41)
6 *a redrawing of boundaries:* the redefinition of accepted categories (line 40)
7 *in line with:* contrary to (line 42)
8 *to give someone the edge:* to give someone a strong advantage (line 69)

❻ Underline the sections of the text referred to by the words and phrases which are boxed in the following extracts.

1 *They said it would never last . . .* (line 1)
2 *. . . which will give you some idea . . .* (lines 5-6)
3 *. . . it meant an apprenticeship of some sort.* (lines 12-13)

4 *In retrospect this was a short-sighted view. . .* (lines 14-15)
5 *This took the form of programmes . . .* (lines 22-3)
6 *. . . which may have included music . . .* (line 27)
7 *. . . sometimes the imagery associated with an experience. . .* (line 32)
8 *Not all of these deal specifically with the music industry.* (line 58)
9 *. . . that is true of other careers as well.* (line 63)
10 *. . . it can give interested people an opportunity to experiment.* (lines 65-6)
11 *This will offer a course of study. . .* (line 73)

❼ Re-read the first ten paragraphs of the text (lines 1-41) and decide which of the following sentences can be added to each paragraph.

1 In fact, music has become big business.
2 If they managed to get a good job when they had finished, then they probably regarded themselves as lucky.
3 Pop/rock music has almost become respectable.
4 If they had realised how things were going to turn out, they might have done something different.
5 Fashion, dance, theatre and the cinema were all influenced by the way that music was developing.
6 This would have been unthinkable.
7 Today there is an entire satellite TV channel devoted to pop/rock music.
8 Writers and singers were aware of the age group that made up the majority of their audience.
9 It has lasted much longer than anyone ever believed possible.
10 They said it was loud and tuneless and they would never listen to it.

❽ For and against

Do you think that colleges of higher education should offer courses like the ones described in the reading text? Working with a partner, write down as many points as you can for and against such courses. Some ideas have been given under each heading.

FOR	AGAINST
● Qualifications are necessary whatever you want to do.	● Pop/rock music is not a proper academic subject.
● The music industry has become so important that it cannot be left in the hands of amateurs.	● Good popular music depends on inspiration, not education.
● Students will be more motivated if courses deal with subjects which they find interesting.	● If colleges offer courses in pop/rock music, employers will not think so highly of their other degrees and diplomas.

❾ Discuss all the points in both lists with your partner and decide what you think. Find another pair in the class whose ideas are different from yours and continue your discussion.

Unit 3

43

VOCABULARY

❸ Match the group noun with the name(s) of the species that belongs to it.

Example: A crowd of people.

a flock of   cows
a shoal of   dogs
a herd of   insects
a pride of   birds or sheep
a swarm of   fish
a pack of   lions

❹ What nouns do you associate with these words? Working in pairs, write full sentences that use them.

group, bunch, cluster, collection, package, series, party, formation

❺ What do you expect to find in the following places? Think of other objects that you could find there.

Example: a library -   normally, books
                      -   could be used to describe a
                          collection of records or CDs

school, gallery, fair, hall, hive, den, arcade, maze

❻ How many of the following orchestral instruments do you recognise? Match the instrument with its name.

clarinet, oboe, flute, horn, tuba, trombone, double-bass, violin, harp, piano, kettledrum, cymbals

❶ Look at the picture and write down all of the words that it makes you think of.

❷ Combine the adjectives and nouns below to complete the headline. How many different headlines could you write? How does the meaning of the headline and its photograph change?

_____ _____ **MARCH THROUGH CITY CENTRE.**

demonstrators   peaceful
youths   violent
hooligans   angry
protestors   dangerous
people   organised
crowds   wild
teachers   harmless
doctors   hungry
students   helpful
pensioners   friendly

7 Working in pairs, list any other musical instruments that you can think of. How can you explain them to someone who doesn't recognise the word?

8 What instruments make these sounds?

*a crash, a bang, a boom,
a whine, a wail, a scream,
a tinkle, a whistle, a twang*

IT'S ONLY ROCK AND ROLL

WRITING

Work in pairs. Look at the images below. Who and what do you recognise? Each of the images can be related to one of the following decades: the 50s, the 60s, the 70s, the 80s or the 90s.

a

b

c

d

e

f

g

h

i

j

k

l

m

n

o

p

Imagine that you have to write a short history of rock and pop music for a children's encyclopaedia. Choose one of the decades and decide which images you would like to use to illustrate your text, then write about the decade.

The following questions may be helpful.

Who were the famous music artists?
What sort of music did they play?
What were the names of their most famous songs?
What other events were happening at the time?
What were the concerns of young people at the time?

PROJECT – THE YOUTH MARKET: A SURVEY

Your class is going to carry out a survey to find out about the 'youth market' in Britain today. Your aim is to collect as much material as you can to produce a report on how manufacturers, advertisers and the media try to attract young people – and how young people react to this.

STAGE ONE: Preparation and research

Before you start to gather information, you will need to decide what areas you are going to investigate and who is going to be responsible for them.

1 In small groups, brainstorm as many different aspects of 'youth culture' as you can. Add your ideas to the spidergrams below and draw further examples for other possible headings.

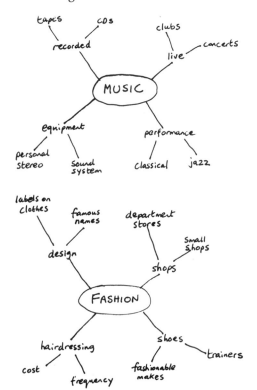

2 Compare your spidergrams with other groups and decide how you are going to focus the survey. Do you want the whole class to concentrate on the same topics and produce a very detailed report? Or would you prefer different groups to find out about different topics and get a broader picture?

3 Use the 'pyramid discussion' technique* to agree on ten main questions that the class would like the project to answer.

> * **'Pyramid discussion' procedure:** First, make your own list of ten questions. Then, with a partner, agree on a common list of ten questions. Next, get together with another pair and again agree on ten questions. Repeat this procedure, with larger and larger groups, until the whole class has reached its agreement.

4 Think about the kinds of information you want and the best people/places to get it from.

Examples:
- newspapers/ magazines
- host families
- advertisements
- music/clothes shops
- local schools/ colleges
- teachers
- local government offices
- public library

5 Decide which groups are going to be responsible for different parts of the survey. Then, in each group, decide how you are going to carry out your research.

Examples:
- in-depth interviews with a few individuals
- brief 'Question-and-Answer' interviews with a wide range of people. (Look back at the guidelines in Unit Two.)
- collection of advertisements (photographs and newspaper cuttings)
- collection of leaflets/brochures
- samples of teenage newspapers/ magazines

6 If you decide to do in-depth interviews, you will need to plan your questions in advance, but also to 'stay on your toes' and be ready for the unexpected. Here are some practical hints to consider before you start. Discuss them in your group and add your own ideas.

- Your interviewee may not understand a question, or may not give as full an answer as you expect. Be ready to ask follow-up questions.

- Some answers may be very different from what you expect. Be ready to respond and to ask extra questions that you have not prepared.

- The whole interview could move in a different direction. You will have to decide whether this is interesting and you want to follow it, or whether you ought to bring it back to the points you had planned to discuss.

- You will probably need time to think about how the interview is developing and possibly to re-think some of your questions. Share the questioning with a partner and give the task of taking notes (or recording the interview) to another member of your group.

STAGE TWO: Planning and editing

The next stage of the project is to analyse all the information you have collected and to think about how you are going to present it in the form of a report.

1   Use the ten main questions which the class agreed on at Stage One as headings to organise your report.

2   Transcription (notes/recordings of interviews). It will probably not be necessary to transcribe all of your interview material. Select extracts from the interviews which relate to the original ten questions.

3   Texts (magazine, newspaper and advertising material). Again, select extracts which are related in some way to your original questions. Concentrate on the way in which language is used to appeal to young readers. How are headlines designed to attract a teenage readership? What key words and phrases are repeated in different texts? What images of youth have you found in photos and other illustrations?

4   Finally, look at the material which you have not used. There may be some interesting information which was not anticipated in the original questions. If necessary, make new headings, so that you can include this extra material.

STAGE THREE: Presentation

Now decide how to present the information you have collected. Consider the following questions:

- Are the group reports going to remain separate or will you put together a single report from the whole class?

- Who is going to read your report(s)? Your teacher? The rest of your class? Other students in the school? Your interviewees?

- Do you want the texts, photos and interview extracts to speak for themselves or will you add some commentary? Or do you want to make the report out of your own writing and photographs, using the material you have collected as illustrations and examples?

REVIEW

PROJECT EVALUATION

How successful was your project? Use the questions below to reflect on how you approached your various tasks, as well as the report(s) you produced.

Preparation and research
How effective was the initial brainstorming activity? Did you find that the spidergram was a useful way of making notes? How easy was it to use the 'pyramid discussion' to arrive at a common list of questions? Did you choose the best people/places to get the information you wanted? What problems did you have when you were interviewing people? How did you deal with them?

Planning and editing
How much transcription did you have to do? Did you find a good variety of texts? How many of your original questions were you unable to answer? How would you try to find those answers if you were doing the project again? Did any new questions appear through the material you collected?

Presentation
Do you think that your final report(s) gave an accurate picture of the young people you met? Are you satisfied with the way that you decided to present your results? What were the reactions of the people who looked at the project?

THINKING ABOUT LANGUAGE LEARNING

Checking your progress

❶ The graph below shows what many people believe is the typical pattern of learning for a student of a foreign language. In pairs, discuss the following questions:

1 Why do most students make such good progress in the early stages of learning a new language?
2 Can you explain the 'plateau' in the centre of this graph?
3 Why do you think advanced students make slower progress than beginners?
4 Does the graph represent your progress in learning English so far? (If not, how would you change it?)
5 Does the graph picture the way you feel your learning should continue in the future? (If not, how would you change it?)

- results of class tests
- examination results
- teacher's comments on written homework
- teacher's comments during lessons
- tutorials (individual discussions) with teacher
- school reports
- making fewer mistakes
- getting what you want in shops, restaurants etc.
- making yourself understood in ordinary conversations
- having to use the dictionary less often when you are reading
- getting more enjoyment from songs, films and TV
- thinking in English
- dreaming in English
- knowing when you have made a mistake and being able to correct it yourself

❷ How do you know that you are making progress? Look at the following ideas and tick (✓) all the ways in which you find you can check your progress. You may also add your own ideas.

❸ Compare your ideas with a partner and discuss the following question:

Who/What gives you most information about your progress?

a tests, exams and homework
b other people (teachers, fellow students, people you meet)
c your own feelings/reflections

READING

4 Working in pairs, make a list of all the things you read in English yesterday.

5 What makes reading in English easier or more difficult? Which of the following statements do you agree with?

- The more I read in a foreign language, the easier it becomes.
- When I pick up a newspaper now, I can get the general sense of most stories and I can understand many of them very well.
- I still find it difficult to read for pleasure, without using a dictionary.
- I find reading in English much easier when I know something about the topic.
- I find that I use different reading techniques for different kinds of texts.
- I need to concentrate when I read in English.
- I find it difficult to continue reading in English for long periods without a break.

6 Look at the list you made for exercise 4. Choose three different kinds of text and discuss the following questions.

1 Why are you reading? (E.g. for general interest, for particular bits of information, for pleasure etc.)

2 What kind of vocabulary do you expect the writer to use?

3 Do you expect the text to be formal (long sentences, difficult grammatical structures, unusual vocabulary) or informal (shorter sentences, simpler grammar, more common vocabulary)?

4 Do you need to understand every sentence in detail or just the general meaning/a few key words?

5 Does the text include any 'signposts' which will help you to follow the message? (E.g. headings, use of different typefaces, underlining etc.)

6 How easy is it to predict what the writer is going to say next?

7 How can you improve your reading comprehension? Discuss the following suggestions and add your own ideas.

- If you want a story to read for pleasure, choose one that you already know – from a translation you have read or a film you have seen.

- Get into the habit of skimming through a newspaper every day. Look out for articles on topics that you are interested in and reserve a little time every day for reading those articles.

- Before you start to read, think about the questions that you want a text to answer. These questions may be about information which you hope the text will give you, or in the case of a story, about the characters, the setting and the plot.

- Try to develop the habit of reading without using a dictionary. Make it a rule only to look up a word if the sense of a paragraph depends on it or if it occurs several times within a text and you cannot guess its meaning from any of the contexts.

REVIEW

In what areas do you feel you have made progress on this course up to now? Think about new things you have learned, as well as areas where you are beginning to feel more confident. Make an individual list of examples and then in small groups, decide on a general list for the class. Use the following headings (and add your own headings, if you wish).

- vocabulary
- idioms
- conversational behaviour
- body language and gestures
- grammar
- listening
- reading
- writing
- study skills
- British life

WRITING

Write a new entry in your learner diary. Look back at what you have written so far and think about the following questions.

1 What have you done/learned since your last entry?
2 Do you feel differently about any of the things you wrote before?
3 Are there any important areas of your experience in Britain which you have not written about yet?
4 What are the things that you will want to remember about this course in six months' time?

❶ Look at the pictures below. What do you think is happening in each picture? What do you think has just happened and what is going to happen?

a

b

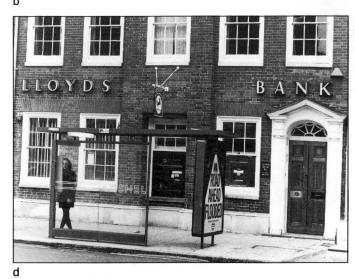

c

d

e

f

g

h

i

j

k

l

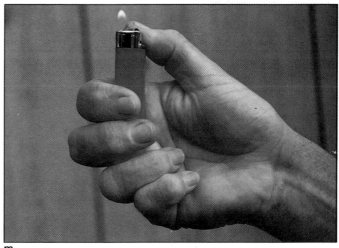

m

❷ Working in pairs, rearrange the pictures into a story.
Decide where the story begins and where it ends. (You
do not have to use all of the pictures.)

❸ Imagine that you are going to publish the story in a
teenage magazine. For each of the photographs in the
sequence that you have chosen, write in supporting
captions, speech bubbles and thought bubbles.

❹ Think about how you would tell the story to the rest of
the class. Make the notes that you would speak from.

❺ Listen to these people being interviewed about stories
and storytelling. While you listen, write down the names
of the stories that they are talking about, then write
down the question that you think the interviewer asked.

SECTION 2

PERSONAL STORIES

❶ Look at the following titles and think of a true story about yourself which you could tell about each of them.

My most embarrassing experience

The most unforgettable person I've ever met

The most frightening moment of my life

A pleasant surprise

The right answer

My biggest mistake

❷ Exchange your ideas with a partner and decide which one of your stories (and which one of your partner's) is the most interesting.

❸ Prepare to tell the story you have selected to the rest of the class. Use the following checklist to help you.

● **Setting**. How long ago did the story take place? At what time of year? Where did it happen? What details of the setting will your listeners need to know? Will you need to describe any important places or things which will be unfamiliar to them?

● **Opening.** How can you get your listeners' attention and make them want to hear your story? What would be the best starting point? Will you need to add any background information?

● **Narration**. What will be the best way to tell the story? Will you simply follow the actual sequence of events? Would it make the story more amusing or more exciting if you changed the sequence? How can you make sure that your listeners want to know what happens next? Are you going to tell the story 'in a straight line' or will you interrupt it?

● **Dialogue.** Can you use direct speech to bring the characters in your story to life? Are there any particular sentences spoken by you or other people which it will be important to remember accurately?

● **Language.** What vocabulary will you need? Are there any words which you are not sure of? What are the connections between different parts of the story? What linking words will you need to help the listener understand these connections? What tenses and other grammatical constructions will be important?

● **Closing.** How are you going to end the story? Have you got a good 'punchline'? Is there a 'moral' – a kind of lesson that you think other people might learn from it? Is the best way of ending the story to return to the beginning?

What I liked

What wasn't clear

What you could do differently

❹ Working in pairs, practise telling your stories. While you listen to your partner, make notes about his/her storytelling technique.

❺ Use your partner's suggestions to improve your story and then tell it to the class.

FOLK TALES AND FAIRY STORIES

❻ Look at the pictures below. Can you think of any stories told in your country in which you can find people and things like these? In small groups, exchange your stories. Do you notice any similarities or connections among the stories? Choose one of them to tell to the rest of the class.

NATIONAL STORIES

❼ What are the stories that the British tell about themselves? Who are their heroes and national figures? What qualities do they admire?

What do you associate with the names and key phrases set out on the right? Use a dictionary to help you and make notes of examples in the spaces provided. (You can add your own ideas, too.)

In small groups, compare your notes. Decide which stories/characters/qualities you think are most typically British and explain your choice to the rest of the class.

❽ What are your national stories? Who are the national figures that everybody knows? How do people in your country describe themselves? Make notes like those in exercise 7. Do students in the class from different countries have the same ideas about your country? Find out what others in your group have written and then compare your results with other groups.

Robin Hood
the Dunkirk spirit
a stiff upper lip
a sense of fair play
King Arthur and the Knights of the Round Table
behaving like a gentleman
Mrs Thatcher
snobbery
patriotism
politeness
support for the underdog
Queen Elizabeth I
tradition

SECTION 3

READING

❶ Before you read the passage discuss the following questions:

Do you read longer passages in English?
How can reading longer passages help to develop your English?
What difficulties do you face when you read a longer passage?
How can you overcome these difficulties?

❷ In the passage below a young girl called Angela describes her life up to the age of thirteen. Relax and read the story from the beginning to the end. While you read it, underline any words or parts of the story that you are not sure about.

MY LIFE STORY

1 The earliest thing I can remember doing occurred when I was four. I was staying with my grandparents and my grandfather and father were going to the 'local' for a drink before dinner. I went with them, riding on the back of Rex, my grandad's dog, who was about three times my size. There is no reason why this should stay in my memory, but it has.

2 Although I cannot remember further back than this, I do know certain things about myself. I was born in East London, where I remained until I was eleven. We lived in one of a row of identical houses, on the first floor of a three-storey house. We had three rooms: a kitchen, a back room and a front room, which was also the bedroom. Our landlady lived on the ground floor. To get to the garden, we had to go through her passage, which she disliked, with the result that I played in the street rather than in the garden, which was overgrown with weeds anyway.

3 Every day, the factories around us poured out clouds of grey-black smoke. This, combined with games which involved crawling through hedges and over walls, made the children in our street look dirty and, according to my father, I was the dirtiest of them all. He said there was never a day when he came home to find me not smeared with dirt and grime, with my hair hanging loose and my frock torn.

4 Although I had plenty of friends, I spent a lot of time on my own. I had a number of dolls and I also had an imaginary friend, called Doris, who always managed to be sitting on a chair whenever one of my parents wanted to sit on it. In bed at night, I used to make up plays about my dolls and fairytale characters and myself, taking all the parts and talking out loud.

5 At four-and-a-half, I started school. I must have been a real problem for some of my teachers. I did not learn to read until fairly late, in spite of the hours spent with my mother in front of the fire, trying to learn the alphabet. For at least eighteen months I could count only as far as five before I got stuck. In my second year in the juniors, I went completely haywire. I dawdled purposely on the way to school; I did not worry much about attending to lessons; I just did not care.

6 By this time I was the leader of a small clique of children. My best friend at the time was Jeannie, in spite of the fact that we quarrelled incessantly. There was always a certain amount of rivalry between us. When playing a game, we always tried to put over our own ideas and, because of this, the games became very much Jeannie's and mine, with the others just doing as they were told. I still made up stories at night, and sometimes during the day, but I was now the proprietor of a hotel. Our bedroom became a dormitory. The living-room was the lounge. The kitchen I split into three strips. The strip where the table was, was the dining-room, the strip with the gas-stove, the kitchen, and the part with the sink, the bathroom. The road outside was a river and the vehicles were boats. Behind a panel in the wall I kept a horse, and a dog slept under my bed.

7 When I was seven, my sister was born. Julie was, and is, as different from me as possible. She hated animals, whereas I loved them. This is odd, because although Julie has never been frightened by an animal, at the age of three I was knocked down by an enormous Alsatian dog. Julie is rarely sentimental, whereas I cry over sad books and films because the characters become so real to me. In the same way, I become angry or happy or puzzled, as the characters do. I often feel a savage satisfaction when a particularly villainous villain is overcome, although I usually dislike violence on television or in films, even if the hero is unhurt. I was a slow starter at school, but Julie knew the alphabet, could write her name and count

54

up to a hundred, all before she started school. Now after being at school for two years, she reads excellently. In fact, our love of books is about the only thing Julie and I share.

8   As I said, during my second year in the junior part of the school, I went mad, but in the third year I settled down again. At the beginning of the fourth year, I took the 'Eleven-Plus'. I had none of the fears about this that the books say we all have and nor did anybody else in my class. I think that this was largely due to our teacher, who explained that it was not a competition, but an assessment. After the examination, things seemed very slack. The time dragged by. At last the results came through. I was to go to a grammar school. Ever since I was a small child, I had dreamed of attending this school.

9   During the summer holiday before I started this school, I nearly went mad with boredom. About half-way through I suddenly contracted an unknown illness. I privately decided that I had poliomyelitis. A vivid imagination can be a handicap. As a little girl I lived in constant fear of a wolf entering the house. Whenever I was on my own, I used to sit at the kitchen table, staring out of the window, so that if a wolf did come through the door, I would not see it. The same imagination which had made every sound into a wolf's footfall now turned every ache into approaching paralysis. But once term started, all my worries cleared up. I was very happy at school, but I had scarcely been there a term and a half when we were offered a flat in Blackheath Village and my parents accepted it.

10   The Friday I left the grammar school, I had no idea where I was to go next. The next Monday I was installed at Kidbrooke Comprehensive School. I liked my new school, although the size of it bewildered me. I was ten minutes late for two lessons in the first week because I got lost. Eventually I became used to the maze of corridors, stairs and floors, and now I find it extremely amusing to see first-formers wandering around in the same predicament that I was once in.

11   About eighteen months ago I suddenly discovered that I liked popular songs and musicians. I started a scrapbook, which, of course, entailed 'wasting' my money on pictures to put into it. Although we had had television ever since Julie was born, we had only one channel, and when we recently bought a television with two, I was plunged into a world where westerns abounded. This had a pronounced effect on the stories which I still make up at night. Now they are about popular singers and television western heroes and I do not figure in them at all.

12   So here I am. At thirteen, not so very different from when I was three, or any other age. I still tell myself stories, even if they have changed in character. I still cry at sad films. I still read books almost indiscriminately. I still spend a lot of time alone. I still enjoy school. I still try to impress my ideas on others. At seven I was going to be an advertiser, a producer or an actress. It has always been something connected with words.

13   Now I would like to be a journalist and I still want, very much, to write a book, although I do not think I have the perseverance. But one can daydream and having daydreamed since I was an infant, I doubt very much if I shall give it up now.

Angela Irene Stratton, 13
award-winning entry, *Daily Mirror*
Children's Literary Competition

❸ After you have read the passage, read the story again with a partner and try to divide it up into sections. Give each section a heading. For example, paragraphs one to five could be called *My earliest memories, life before school.*

❹ If there are still some words or expressions in the passage that you are not sure about, but which you think are very important to understand, ask others in the class to help you.

❺ The story contains many images that are particularly British. Look at the words and expressions below. How many do you recognise? How would you explain them to someone who has never been to Britain?

the local
the row of houses
the landlady
the juniors
the comprehensive school

WRITING

❻ Think about your early memories. List seven experiences that you remember from your very early childhood until the age of sixteen.

❼ For each of the incidents make further notes:

- where did it happen, what details of the setting do you remember?
- when did it happen?
- who were you with?
- what were the people like, what details do you remember?
- what does the incident reveal about your character?

❽ Now limit yourself to five of the incidents and write your own story. When you have finished, circulate the stories around the class for everyone to read. At the bottom of each story write either one comment that gives praise or one question about the story.

SECTION 4

LANGUAGE PRACTICE

LINKING WORDS

❶ Contrasts

Look at the following sets of sentences. What differences do you notice about the way that they are formed? Are there any differences in meaning? Do any of the sentences seem particularly formal or informal?

1 His parents were uneducated, but he went to university.
Although his parents were uneducated, he went to university.
He went to university, although his parents were uneducated.

2 She spent a lot of time alone, although she had plenty of friends.
In spite of having plenty of friends, she spent a lot of time alone.
In spite of the fact that she had a lot of friends, she spent a lot of time alone.
Despite having a lot of friends, she spent a lot of time alone.
Despite the fact that she had a lot of friends, she spent a lot of time alone.

3 She speaks French fluently, although she has never been to France.
She speaks French fluently, though she has never been to France.
She speaks French fluently, even though she has never been to France.

4 He passed the exam, but his brother failed.
He passed the exam, whereas his brother failed.

❷ Complete the following sentences, using *but, although, despite, even though* or *whereas*. If you are not sure about the correct answer, try saying the sentence aloud to a partner and see how it sounds. (In some cases, more than one answer is possible.)

1 _____ being a late starter, Angela became a successful student.
2 She found reading difficult at first, _____ her mother had tried to teach her.
3 Angela was sometimes late for school, _____ her sister was always on time.
4 _____ she had some problems at first, she soon settled down.
5 _____ she was very happy, she had to move to a new school.
6 She loves animals, _____ her unpleasant experience with the Alsatian.
7 She would like to become a writer, _____ she says this is just a dream.

8 _____ the fact that she is a teenager, she still cries at sad films.
9 She still tells herself stories, _____ the character of the stories has changed.
10 Her ambitions have changed, _____ they are still connected with words.

❸ Reasons and results

Think about the connections between the sentence in the box below and each of the sentences around it. Which are reasons and which are results? Join them to the sentence in the box, using *because* or *with the result that*.

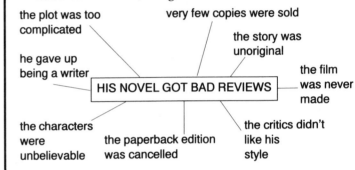

the plot was too complicated

very few copies were sold

he gave up being a writer

the story was unoriginal

HIS NOVEL GOT BAD REVIEWS

the film was never made

the characters were unbelievable

the paperback edition was cancelled

the critics didn't like his style

❹ Complete the following statements about your own reasons for doing things and the results of things you have done.

1 I started learning English _____
2 I didn't always work hard at school _____
3 I sometimes misunderstand things I hear in English _____
4 I want to improve my English _____
5 I'd like/wouldn't like to visit the United States _____
6 I've learnt a lot about British life _____

❺ Purpose

Underline the word(s) used to express the purpose of the action in each of the following sentences. Which expressions do you think are formal/less formal?

1 Parents read their children bedtime stories to help them get to sleep.
2 I read novels for entertainment.
3 I won't tell you how the story ends so as not to spoil your enjoyment.
4 He told the story in the present tense so as to make it more exciting.
5 She decided to write detective stories so that she would reach a wide audience.
6 Some writers use fables in order to teach us how to behave.
7 This is a true story, but some names have been changed in order not to cause embarrassment.

❻ Use your own ideas to complete the following sentences.

1 A good storyteller uses humour to _____
_____

2 In order to tell a good story, you need _____
_____

3 Many people read short stories for _____
_____

4 I'll tell you a story so as to _____
_____

5 He tells the story differently each time in order not to
_____

6 She always describes the setting in great detail so as to
_____

7 I'm often reading two or three books at the same time
so as not to _____

❼ Relative clauses

Complete the following table:

_____	refers to a place
_____	used without a noun before it
_____	refers to time
which	_____
that	_____
_____	refers to a person (sentence subject)
whom	_____

❽ Add your own ideas to complete the following story frame. (You can also add further sentences between those in the frame.)

It all began in _____ where _____
_____ . The first time I _____
_____ was on the day when _____
_____ . I had noticed _____
_____ , which I thought was very
strange. The man who _____ was
called_____ . He was the same man
who _____ . What surprised·me
was _____ . He said something to
me that _____ , but which _____
_____ . It was _____
_____ that made me realise how
_____ . I wasn't sure whose
_____ , but I was determined to
find out what _____ . The thing
which really _____ was _____
_____ . I'll never know how much
_____ or who _____
_____ .

❾ Defining and non-defining relative clauses

Look at the relative clauses in the following sentences. Do they add essential or extra information? Is it possible to remove them without leaving the sentence incomplete or changing the meaning? Which of the sentences would be more likely to be spoken/written?

1 This is a book for people who enjoy adventure stories.
2 Conrad, who was born in Poland, wrote all his novels in English.
3 I heard the story from my father, who had heard it from his father.
4 The story of Cinderella, which every child knows, was written by a Frenchman.
5 Children like to hear stories that they know.
6 The Booker Prize, which is Britain's best-known literary award, has twice been shared between two writers.
7 I can't remember the name of the writer who won the Booker Prize last year.
8 His biography, which was called *My Life,* was a best-seller
9 The writer whose books I enjoy most is Agatha Christie.
10 Agatha Christie, whose detective stories are enjoyed by people all over the world, is still one of Britain's most popular writers.

❿ Match the sentence halves below and join them up, using one of the following linking expressions. (You can check the original sentences in Angela's life story in Section 3.)

*although   where   with the result that   but   ever since
in spite of the fact that   before   even if   whereas   when
so that   because*

I was born in East London	I loved them.
She disliked us going through the passage	I remained until I was eleven.
I could only count as far as five	we quarrelled incessantly.
My best friend was Jeannie	a particularly villainous villain is overcome.
I still made up stories	I played in the street.
She hated animals	the hero is unhurt.
I often feel a savage satisfaction	I would not see the wolf coming through the door.
I usually dislike violence on television	I got lost.
I had dreamed of attending this school	I got stuck.
I liked my new school	now I was the proprietor of a hotel.
I used to stare out of the window	I was a small child.
I was ten minutes late	the size of it bewildered me.

⓫ Write your own short 'life story' (maximum: 300 words). Try to make use of some of the linking phrases in exercise 10 and include as many of the following points as you can:

● brief description of where you grew up
● contrasts between different houses/flats you have lived in
● contrasts between different schools you have attended
● the reasons for any important changes in your life
● the results of any important decisions you've taken
● the purpose of any study/training

SECTION 5

RECORDING A LIFE

❶ Work in pairs and list all of the ways that you can keep a record of your life, (e.g. photograph albums, diaries...).

❷ Now list all of the ways that others have kept a record of you.

❸ Look at all of the texts below. Identify each one then decide who produced each text and who it was produced for.

DK 123456

CERTIFIED COPY of an
Pursuant to the Births and

ENTRY OF BIRTH.
Deaths Registration Act, 1953

Registration District	BISHOPS STORTFORD						COUNTY OF HERTFORDSHIRE		
1969 Birth in the Sub-district of			BISHOPS STORTFORD			in the			
Columns	1	2	3	4	5	6	7	8	9	10
No.	When and where born	Name	Sex	Name. and surname of father	Name. surname, and maiden surname of mother	Occupation of father	Signature, description and residence of informant	When registered	Signature of registrar	Name entered after registration
246	Eighteenth June, 1969, Herts and Essex General Hospital, Bishops Stortford.	Anna Rose WINSTANLEY	Female	Peter Edward WINSTANLEY	Laura Alice HOBBES	Train driver	Laura Alice Hobbes, Mother, 3 Westbury House, Stortford Road, Dunmow.	Eighteenth June, 1969	A.H. Field Registrar	

Registrar of Births and Deaths for the Sub-district of BISHOPS STORTFORD., in the COUNTY OF HERTFORDSHIRE
WITNESS MY HAND this 18th day of June 1969.

A Summary C.V.

Name: Anna Rose Winstanley
Date of birth: 18 June, 1969
Marital status: Single

PROFESSIONAL QUALIFICATIONS:
1987 Heath Mead Comprehensive School
- 'A' Levels: French (A)
  Spanish (A)
  English (B)
1991 South London University
- B.A. French and Spanish (2i)
1990 The Ball School of Languages
- Certificate in Teaching English as a Foreign Language

PROFESSIONAL EXPERIENCE:
- June 1993 to present: translator for Eurogen, specialising in contracts and technical specifications.
- September 1991 to June 1993: teacher of English in The Little English School in Seville. Taught at all levels from beginner to advanced.
- September 1991 to June 1993: freelance translator and interpreter.
- September 1990 to June 1991: assistant at the Lycée in Romorantin, France.

FURTHER RELEVANT INFORMATION:
- During my second year at university, I served as Secretary for the Student Union and developed the E. Mail student magazine link with universities in France, Spain and Uruguay.
- September 1991. Entered the open competition to work as a General Administrator in the European Commission and achieved the third stage.
- Computer literacy: am able to use Word and Pagemaker for word-processing and desk-top publishing and am familiar with using a variety of database and spread-sheet software.
- Am a competent speaker and reader of Russian and am currently attending classes in Japanese.
- My leisure interests include film, hang-gliding and antique bookbinding.

HEATH MEAD COMPREHENSIVE – School Report

ENGLISH LANGUAGE AND LITERATURE	Anna is an outstanding student with originality and a flair in her writing. She reads with a passion, devouring books in a couple of days. She joins in class discussion well and encourages others.
MATHEMATICS	A good all-rounder, but Anna must pay more attention to detail if she is to get the higher marks. Her work in algebra is sound, but her work in statistics is shaky. She grasps the basic concepts, but does not check the figures.
SCIENCE	Anna has made considerable progress this year, although she almost managed to blow up the laboratory during the hydrogen project, she is thorough and careful in her approach to experimental work.
ART	Anna has an excellent understanding of the history of Italian art during the Renaissance and her life drawing is improving slowly
HISTORY	A lively and enthusiastic student who is a pleasure to teach. She obtained very high marks for her essay on the origins of the First World War.
SPANISH	A very communicative pupil. She should consider following a career that makes use of her talents for other languages. She claims to be enjoying her reading of Lorca
PHYSICAL EDUCATION	Anna has ability, but prefers to play alone. She could become a good hockey player, but she doesn't really seem to enjoy team sports.
FORM TUTOR'S REPORT	This has been another year of success for Anna. She is a valuable member of the school who contributes with enthusiasm. She is a good junior librarian and was a member of the team that won the local schools' debating competition. Congratulations. The report shows good progress and promises much for the years ahead.

TO WHOM IT MAY CONCERN

Ms Winstanley came to us in 1993 with high academic credentials and proven experience as a teacher. She settled into the company quickly and is an extremely competent and confident translator. We trust her to work with the most sensitive and complicated material. She behaves with the ease of a diplomat when she is entertaining French and Spanish partners and has been involved as an interpreter on several occasions.

Her Spanish is perhaps a little stronger than her French and she seems to be very much 'at home' in the culture of southern Spain where she spent time as a student and then later working teaching English.

Ms Winstanley has excellent relationships with others in her team and is known to be reliable and co-operative. She is never late with her deadlines and can work under pressure. She is ambitious, but not 'cut-throat' in her approach. We wish her all the best in any job applications that she may be making and have made it clear to her that there is a career structure within the company through which she would progress at speed if she chooses to remain with Eurogen.

L. James

L. James
Senior Personnel Manager
Eurogen

...VERSITY OF SOUTH LONDON

This is to certify that

Anna Rose Winstanley

*after having satisfied all the conditions
prescribed in respect
of the Statutes of the University
was on the* twenty-first *day of* January
duly admitted to the Degree of

BACHELOR OF ARTS

As witness my hand this twenty-fourth *day of* January 1991

Assistant Registrar

YOUTH HOSTELS ASSOCIATION
(England & Wales)
MEMBERSHIP CARD

(Membership No.) (Date of Birth) (Category of Membership)

5432   18/6/69   STUDENT

Date Paid 26/12/90

EXPIRES END   12/91

1990 YHF 1991

CARD NOT VALID UNTIL OFFICIALLY STAMPED

---

❹ Use the information in the texts to discuss the following statements. Decide whether it is true or false, partly true or we can't tell because there is not enough evidence. Rewrite some of the sentences to make them clearer.

1 Anna succeeded in all of her subjects while she was at school.
2 Her love of modern languages came from her father.
3 Anna was born at home in 1969.
4 Religious Education and French were probably her favourite school subjects.
5 Anna seems to be a thoroughly extrovert character who doesn't like to be alone. This is proved by her leisure interests and school habits.
6 The company she works for doesn't really think that she has much chance of getting a better job inside 'Eurogen'.
7 She is the sort of person who would enjoy a holiday lying around on a beach and relaxing all day.
8 At work she does not get on very well with colleagues because of her aggressive approach.
9 Her experience suggests that she is sensitive to the customs and lifestyles in countries outside Britain.
10 Anna is the sort of person who would be interesting to meet.

WRITING

❺ In not more than 150 words, summarise the character of Anna as you understand her.

OBITUARIES AND EPITAPHS

❻ Obituaries (written accounts of a person's life that immediately follow her/his death) and gravestones also record people's lives. Hunt through the papers and local churchyards for good examples!

VOCABULARY

FAMILY RELATIONSHIPS

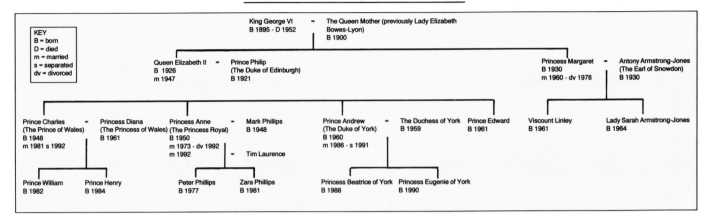

KEY
B = born
D = died
m = married
s = separated
dv = divorced

King George VI
B 1895 - D 1952
= The Queen Mother (previously Lady Elizabeth Bowes-Lyon)
B 1900

Queen Elizabeth II
B 1926
m 1947
= Prince Philip
(The Duke of Edinburgh)
B 1921

Princess Margaret
B 1930
m 1960 - dv 1978
= Antony Armstrong-Jones
(The Earl of Snowdon)
B 1930

Prince Charles
(The Prince of Wales)
B 1948
m 1981 s 1992
= Princess Diana
(The Princess of Wales)
B 1961

Princess Anne
(The Princess Royal)
B 1950
m 1973 - dv 1992
m 1992
= Mark Phillips
B 1948

= Tim Laurence

Prince Andrew
(The Duke of York)
B 1960
m 1986 - s 1991
= The Duchess of York
B 1959

Prince Edward
B 1961

Viscount Linley
B 1961

Lady Sarah Armstrong-Jones
B 1964

Prince William
B 1982

Prince Henry
B 1984

Peter Phillips
B 1977

Zara Phillips
B 1981

Princess Beatrice of York
B 1988

Princess Eugenie of York
B 1990

❶ Look at this famous family tree, then use the right word from the list to complete the following statements.

wife, husband, son, daughter, nephew, niece, aunt, uncle, engaged, married, separated, divorced, grandmother, grandfather, grandchildren, widower, widow, bachelor, spinster, cousin, mother-in-law, father-in-law, son-in-law

1 The Queen Mother has two children and six _____ .
2 Prince Andrew is _____ from The Duchess of York.
3 Princess Margaret has three _____, Charles, Andrew and Edward, and one _____, Anne.
4 Viscount Linley is Prince Charles' _____ .
5 Antony Armstrong-Jones and Princess Margaret are _____ .
6 King George VI died in 1952, leaving Lady Elizabeth Bowes-Lyon a _____ with two children when she was 52 years old.
7 Prince Edward is a _____ .
8 The six royal grandchildren have five _____ and four _____ .

❷ Discussion

People often hold very strong opinions about the Royal Family. Read the following statements and underline the words that are used to present an argument or show the person's feelings; decide what kind of person was speaking and then discuss the arguments for and against keeping a royal tradition.

MARY
Oh I wouldn't want them to go, I think they do a good job for the country, I really do, definitely, I follow them all the time and I am proud to say that I once met Princess Anne.

RICHARD
Although you may not agree with me, I have to confess that I believe the Royal Family to be a complete and utter waste of taxpayers' money. It is an unjust society that pays to keep that sort of wealth with one family, I mean, we're talking about something like three million pounds a year to subsidise them... it's a disgrace...

JUDY
Well, there are clear cases both for and against keeping the monarchy, but in their favour, you have to admit that they are a good tourist attraction, they have important diplomatic responsibilities, they encourage a more caring attitude through the good works that they do in poorer countries and above all else, they are the best living soap opera...

SIMON
It is a question of tradition, they are part of the country's heritage, its past, its character, deep down everyone who is British wants them, we love them in a strange way, even if we love to hate them, they help to make us different, certainly I would hate to see them go, to be honest with you, I'd like to meet them but I suppose they are just ordinary people underneath it all, just like you and me...

PHIL

I don't know really, I'm in two minds about them, but I suppose if I have to commit myself then I would keep them, I think they do a good job and in the long run what do we gain by getting rid of them?

0 – 10

11 – 20

21 – 30

31 – 40

41 – 50

51 – 60

61 – 70

WRITING

❸ Decide what you think about royalty. In not more than 200 words, summarise your feelings and explain your opinions.

❹ All of the following words are used to speak about age. Work in pairs and use the chart to help you rearrange them into an order. You may find it difficult to decide exactly where to place some of the words.

youth, old age, secondary school age, middle-aged, in her/his twenties, pensioner, heading for retirement, new-born, primary school age, adult, baby, infant, teenage, toddler, student, adolescent, mature, child

❺ Find the odd man out.

- *landlady, lodger, guest, hotel, resident, occupant*
- *terraced house, bungalow, semi-detached house, bed-sit, three-storey house*
- *haywire, thankful, mad, confused, crazy, strange*
- *dawdle, stroll, march, walk, run*
- *clique, hairband, club, group, gang, team*
- *weeds, orchard, crops, flowers, plantation*

❻ Work in pairs and divide the animals listed below into three groups under the headings in the table. **Note:** sometimes it might be difficult to decide which heading(s) to use.

cat, dog, horse, donkey, lion, giraffe, hamster, pig, goat, sheep, bear, wolf, fox

Add other animals, fish and birds to your lists.

Domestic animals and pets	Working animals and farm animals	Wild animals

❼ Decide which animals make the following noises;

purr, growl, grunt, bark, squeal, neigh, bleat, roar

END-OF-COURSE PROJECT

Project work has been an important feature of this course. Projects have given you opportunities to work together outside the classroom, using English for a *real* purpose. When you work on a project, you are not being told by a teacher or a coursebook what language to use – you are making your own *real* choices. Projects give you the chance to develop more confidence about using your *own* English.

By now you should have learned quite a lot about your class, the school and the local environment. In this final project, the choices are all yours – *you* decide on the topic, the project teams and the methods of working.

When choosing a topic, think first about what you will find interesting, but remember that you are going to present it to the rest of the class (or the rest of the school) at the end of the course – so think about your audience, too. Whatever you decide to do, it should be something that will challenge you to make even greater use of your English than you have before – for *real* communication.

Here are some suggestions:

1 A CLASS MAGAZINE

Prepare, produce and publish an end-of-course magazine. (This will be particularly useful if you want a chance to practise writing in English.)

● Your magazine might include some of the following features:

- an editorial: an introduction which tells your readers about the magazine and describes the contents
- articles about people's experiences during the course
- interviews with students, teachers and other members of staff
- extracts from students' diaries
- reviews of films, plays etc.
- poems, jokes and stories
- letters from students in other groups
- photographs, drawings and cartoons

● When you are planning the magazine, think about these points:

- **layout:** size and number of pages
- **text:** typed, handwritten or a mixture of both?
- **cover design:** photographs, drawings, headlines or a combination?
- **content:** sequence and arrangement of different features
- **cost:** if everyone in the school buys a copy, how much will you have to charge to cover the cost of photocopying?
- **distribution:** central sales point or members of the group taking copies around the school?

2 STORY-TELLING

Select some well-known folk-tales and fairy stories from various parts of the world and present them to the rest of the class. (This will probably be more successful with a group of four or more people.)

● You might begin to make your selection in one of the following ways:

- **Story-swapping.** Exchange stories which have similar characters or a similar theme. (The same stories are often found in different countries.)
- **Story dominoes.** Each person in the group tells a story which has some kind of connection with the previous one.
- **Do-it-yourself stories.** Choose a number of typical things from famous stories and use them to make up your own tales. (E.g. princess, magician, castle, journey, monster, forest, battle, gold, happy ending.)

● Think about different ways of presenting different stories, using a variety of media. Here are some ideas:

- a poster display, telling the story in the form of a strip cartoon or a wall newspaper
- a traditional story-telling session, in which each member of the group takes part in *telling* the story (not reading it)
- a dramatic presentation, with dialogue for all the characters or with a narrator who tells the story and actors who mime
- a video film, using costumes, make-up and outside locations

3 THE CLASS DRAMA PERFORMANCE

Rehearse and perform a short sketch or one-act play. (This would be an ideal contribution to an end-of-course party.)

● First, decide whether you are going to perform an existing script or whether you are going to write something yourselves. Your teacher will be able to recommend collections of suitable sketches or one-act plays, but you may find it more satisfying to write your own. This is often more challenging, of course, but it means that you can make use of situations and characters from the course itself, which might be more entertaining for your audience!

● If you decide to write your own sketch, you may find it useful to think about the following:

- **Length.** A short sketch that makes its point clearly and amusingly: get the audience's attention and keep them interested.

- **Dialogue.** Keep it short and simple: make sure that it can be understood and enjoyed by everyone.
- **Costumes and set.** These do not have to be very complicated, but it is helpful to have one or two recognisable visual signals for the audience.

● Decide when you are going to give your performance and design a poster to advertise it.

4 RECORDED INTERVIEWS

Prepare and record a series of interviews with people inside and outside the school.

● Decide which topic(s) will add to your knowledge of life in Britain.

● You may wish to ask a few questions to a large number of people from different backgrounds, or you may prefer to carry out longer interviews with just one or two people.

● Practise using the tape recorder before you start and think about the best places to conduct the interviews.

● Edit the tape, if necessary, using a double-cassette player or the school language laboratory.

● Write a listener's guide to accompany your recordings. This might include:

  - an introduction, explaining what you wanted to find out
  - information about the recordings – dates, times and places; names, ages and occupations of interviewees
  - photographs of interviewees
  - a list of the main questions asked
  - notes of some of the main points in the answers. (Don't try to write down the whole interview!)

● Other students will probably want a copy of your tape – so give yourself enough time.

5 A VIDEO FILM

Make a short video film which in some way summarises your image and experience of life in Britain.

● Plan your filming programme. If you do not have editing equipment, you will have to make sure that the sequence of filming is the same sequence that you want in the finished film.

● If you are going to reconstruct or retell any events, use the 'storyboard' technique: draw a series of sketches (like a strip cartoon) to represent a series of camera shots.

● Write an introduction, explaining the background to the film.

● Other students will probably want a copy of your tape – so give yourself enough time.

NOTES:
(1) If you or the school do not have a video camera, there are hire facilities in most towns.
(2) Video recordings made in Britain which can be shown on a British television cannot always be used with video recorders in other countries.

6 THE SCHOOL PROSPECTUS

Prepare and produce a school prospectus, giving your view of what it is like to be a student at your school.

● Read the regular school prospectus or course brochure and see how it works as publicity material.

● Look at other brochures and publicity material and see how language, layout and visual material is used to attract the reader.

7 A SCHOOL GAME

Prepare a board game (like *Monopoly)* based on the experiences of a student visiting Britain for a course like yours.

● Look at some real board games to give you some ideas and to see the kind of language used.

● These are some features which you might include:

  - cards which players have to read if they land on a particular place on the board and which give them good news or bad news (e.g. *You have a record played on the local radio station. Advance three spaces.* Or *You leave your homework on the bus. Miss a turn.)*
  - choices (e.g. two different routes, one which is safe but slow and one which is shorter, but may be difficult.)
  - language tasks (e.g. grammar questions, spelling etc.)

● Write the rules for playing the game – and play it yourselves to make sure that it works.

8 A SPECIAL STUDY

You may wish to find out more about some area(s) of British life, or to learn something about one of the many subjects that have not been covered in this book.

● Possible subject areas might include: the Royal Family; British politics; popular culture; the arts in Britain; sport and leisure; the environment; trade, industry and the economy; Britain's relationships with other countries.

Decide on your own project. Decide who you would like to work with and how you will carry out your project.

REVIEW

LOOKING BACK...AND LOOKING AHEAD

This final Review gives you the opportunity to reflect on your stay in Britain and what you have learned, as well as looking ahead to your future language learning.

❶ Complete the following questionnaire.

Section 1: Britain and the British

1   What impression did you have of the country and the people *before you came to Britain?* Make a note of the most appropriate adjectives under each heading.

Britain	The British

2   Have your opinions changed? Which adjectives would you want to change? Are there any that you would like to add?

3   What images and experiences will you remember most? What have you heard/seen/read that will stay in your mind?

4   What are the things which you now feel are most 'typically British'?

5   What souvenirs have you bought/will you buy for yourself and for your family and friends?

6   What have been your most positive/negative experiences?

7   What advice would you give to a friend who was planning to come to Britain for a similar length of time?

Section 2: Language Learning

1   In what areas (e.g. vocabulary, grammar, pronunciation) has your *knowledge* of English improved during the course?

2   In what ways have your *language skills* (i.e. listening, reading, speaking, writing) improved?

3   In what *situations* do you now feel more confident about using the language?

4   How has your English improved (a) inside the classroom and (b) outside the classroom?

Inside	Outside

5   What can you do in English that you could not do before/better than you could do before?

Could not do before	Can now do better

Section 3: The Course

1   How easy/difficult did you find the different parts of the course? Choose the appropriate point on each of the lines below and mark it with a cross (x).

	very easy _____ very difficult
reading texts	_____
listening tasks	_____
oral practice	_____
written work	_____
project work	_____
language study	_____
vocabulary	_____
thinking about language learning	_____
other (please give details)	_____

2   Which parts of the course did you find:
a most enjoyable _____
least enjoyable? _____
b most interesting _____
least interesting _____
c most useful _____
least useful _____

3   Imagine that you are planning a short language course for students like yourself. What would you

include in the programme? What would you leave out?

❷ Compare your questionnaire with a partner. Which questions have you answered differently? Ask your partner to explain his/her answers.

❸ Work in small groups. Give a brief report to the group of *your partner's* ideas. Then discuss the question below. Choose a secretary to take notes and a group representative to report back to the whole class.

1 When people at home ask you to describe Britain and the British, what will you say?

2 What are the special advantages of following a short language course in the country where the language is spoken?

3 What recommendations would you make to a new student who wanted to get the most out of a short course in Britain?

❹ You are going to hear three students explaining how they tried to keep up their English and go on learning when they got home. Listen and decide which of their strategies you will try to follow after this course. Make notes in the spaces below while you listen.

SPEAKER 1

SPEAKER 2

SPEAKER 3

❺ In small groups, discuss the ideas described on the tape and explain why you think you would/would not find them useful.

WRITING

❻ Choose one of the following tasks.

1 Write a short report about the course (to be read by your employer or teacher). The report should include the following:

● **Introduction:** a brief description of the school, the timetable and your fellow students.

● **Summary:** what you feel you have learned during the course. (Think about life in Britain as well as language learning – in the classroom and outside.)

● **Evaluation:** positive and negative features of the experience.

● **Conclusion:** your overall judgement.

2 Write a letter to an English-speaking friend, describing your experience in Britain. Tell your friend:

● what you were expecting the course to be like

● how you felt when you first arrived in Britain

● how your ideas/feelings changed during the course

● how you are feeling now

3 Write a personal language learning plan for the next six months. Explain how you are going to continue to improve your English. Try to comment on the following:

● using the new vocabulary I have learned

● remembering new grammatical structures and using them

● reading and listening to real English

● practising spoken English

● writing in English

COURSE DIARY

The following pages are for you to write your own learning diary during the course. The diary will provide you with an interesting personal record of the course and will be helpful in various ways. You can:

- describe your most memorable experiences;
- keep a record of your learning – about both language and culture;
- write about the process of learning – which lessons and which activities you find interesting and useful;
- write about your feelings at different moments during the course;
- make notes (in the space on the right-hand side of each page) of particular words and expressions that you want to remember.

You don't have to make a diary entry every day – two or three times a week will probably be enough, but set aside definite times and give yourself at least half an hour for writing.

The diary will give you the opportunity to write freely in English. It can be absolutely private and you don't have to show it to anyone, but you may wish your teacher to see it. If you do show it to your teacher, decide whether you want your mistakes to be corrected or whether you just want replies and comments on the content.

The diary pages contain a few headings and suggestions to help you, but you can add your own headings and you can also decide how you want to organise the page space.

ARRIVAL AND FIRST IMPRESSIONS

- Expectations, hopes and fears: *what I think the course will be like.*
- First impressions: *what has (not) surprised me.*
- Personal objectives: *what I want to have learned by the end of the course.*

Words and expressions to remember

IMPRESSIONS WEEK BY WEEK

The next four pages are for you to record your impressions and reflections as you work through the course. You may wish to answer some of the following questions:

● What have I been able to understand without great difficulty?
● Which lessons/activities have I found most stimulating/useful?
● What do I still feel uncertain about?
● How have my feelings and opinions changed?

UNIT 1

Words and expressions to remember

LOOKING BACK . . .

- What have I learned – about the language, the culture and about my own style of learning?
- What have I enjoyed doing most and how has it helped me to learn?
- What will I remember most clearly?

Words and expressions to remember

Course Diary

... AND LOOKING AHEAD

- How will I be able to remember what I have learned?
- How will I go on learning in the future?
- How will I keep my English fresh?

Words and expressions to remember

Grammar Summary

Grammar Summary

This is a basic summary of the general grammatical areas contained in the three levels of the MACMILLAN SHORT COURSE PROGRAMME. It is designed for reference by the learner, and serves to reinforce the language practice done in class.

For detailed explanations of grammar points, consult a reference grammar. For further grammatical practice, use a good grammar practice book.

1 VERBS

1.1 THE VERB 'TO BE'

Affirmative:
Note the contraction of subject and verb:
I'm, She's, We're, etc.

I'm thirteen.
He's hungry.
They're in Scotland.

Negative:
Add *not* after the verb:

You are *not* Spanish.

We can also use the contracted form:

She *isn't* hungry.
You *aren't* at home.

Interrogative:
We make this form by putting the verb before the subject:

Is he Spanish?
Is she thirteen?
Are you hungry?

The **past tense** of the verb *to be* is formed in the same way, using *was* and *were*:

I was	We were
You were	You were
He/She/It was	They were

The **negative** and **interrogative** forms are made in the same way as the present tense:

Negative:	I was not/wasn't	We were not/weren't
Interrogative:	Was I?	Were we?

SUMMARY: VERB 'TO BE' PRESENT AND PAST TENSES

AFFIRMATIVE

I	am 'm	was	Spanish.
He She It	is 's	was	thirteen. hungry.
You We They	are 're	were	at home.

NEGATIVE

I	am not 'm not	was not (wasn't)	Spanish.
He She It	is not isn't	was not (wasn't)	thirteen. hungry.
You We They	are not aren't	were not (weren't)	at home.

INTERROGATIVE

Am Was	I	Spanish?
Is Was	he she it	thirteen?
		hungry?
Are Were	you we they	at home?

1.2 THE VERB 'TO HAVE GOT'

Affirmative   We normally use the contracted form:

> *I've got* a stereo.
> *She's got* brown hair.

Negative: We put *not (n't)* after have:

> You *haven't got* a stereo.
> He *hasn't got* any biscuits.

Interrogative: We put the verb *have* before the subject:

> *Have we got* any biscuits?
> *Has he got* a stereo?

The past tense is formed with *had* in the same way.

Affirmative: All the forms use *had*.
The contracted form of *had* is *'d*.

> I *had* got   We *had* got
> I*'d* got   We*'d* got

Negative: She had not got   They had not got
She hadn't got   They hadn't got

Interrogative: Had he got?   Had they got?

AFFIRMATIVE

I You We They	have 've had 'd	got	a stereo.
			brown hair.
He She It	has 's had 'd		some biscuits.

NEGATIVE

I You We They	have not haven't had not hadn't	got	a stereo.
			brown hair.
He She It	has not hasn't had not hadn't		any biscuits.

Have	I you we they	got	a stereo? brown hair?
Has	he she it		any biscuits?

1.3 MODAL AUXILIARIES ('CAN', 'COULD', 'MUST', 'SHOULD', 'MIGHT')

These verbs have several special features:

- They have no infinitive form.
- The verb after the auxiliary drops *to*.
- All present tense forms are identical.

> She can play the piano.
> They could swim.

CAN

Affirmative: We use the pronoun + modal:
I, You, He, She, It, We, They *can*

Negative: We normally add *n't* in spoken English; we often use *not* in written or formal English:

> *He can't* ride a bike.
> *You can't* play the piano.

Interrogative: We put *can* before the subject:

> *Can* I swim this afternoon?
> *Can* he ride a bike?

COULD

Past tense: The past tense of *can* is *could*.

Affirmative: I, You, He, She, It, We, They *could*

Negative: We use *couldn't* or *could not*.

Interrogative: *Could* I, you, he, she, we, they?

Note: We use *can* and *could* to express ability.
We also use *could* to speak about possible future actions:

> We *could* play tennis tomorrow.

MUST

Must is only used in the present tense.

Affirmative: She *must* go home at eight.
They *must* study.

Negative: You *mustn't (must not)* come back late.
He *mustn't (must not)* ride a bike.

Interrogative: *Must* you play your stereo tonight?

Note: We use *must* to express an urgent need.
We also use *must* to give orders.

SHOULD
All forms of the verb are the same.

Affirmative: She *should* study harder.

Negative: He *shouldn't* (should not) swim today.

Interrogative: *Should* I talk to her?

Note: We use *should* to express obligation.
We also use *should* to give advice.

MIGHT
Might is the past tense of *may*.
All forms of the verb are the same.

Affirmative: She *might* be at home.

Negative: They *mightn't (might not)* come this afternoon.

Interrogative: *Might* we go to London tomorrow?

Note: We use *might* to express a possibility in the present.

MODAL AUXILIARIES (CAN, COULD, MUST, SHOULD, MIGHT)

AFFIRMATIVE

I You	can	play the piano.
He She It	could must	swim.
You We They	should might	ride a bike.

NEGATIVE

I You	can't couldn't mustn't	play the piano.
He She It	shouldn't	swim.
You We They	should not mightn't might not	ride a bike.

INTERROGATIVE

Can Could	I you he	play the piano?
Must	she it	swim?
Should	you we	ride a bike?
Might	they	

1.4 The Simple Present tense

Affirmative: We make the Simple Present tense with the infinitive without *to*. The form is the same except for the third person singular, where we add *'s'*.

> I work.
> He, She, It works.

Negative: We use the verb *to do* as an auxiliary with the main verb.

> I *do* not *(don't)* work.
> She *does* not *(doesn't)* work.

Interrogative: We use the verb *to do* as an auxiliary before the main verb, and we put the subject after the auxiliary:

> *Do* you work?
> *Does* he work?

Note: We use the Simple Present for actions we do habitually or regularly.
>   I come to Britain every year.

1.5 The Simple Past tense

We make the Simple Past tense of regular verbs by adding *-ed* to the infinitive. All persons have the same form.

> I, You, He, She, It, We, They work*ed*.

If the infinitive ends in *-e*, we just add *-d*.

> like ... lik*ed*

If the infinitive ends in *-y*, we drop the *-y* and add *-ied*.

> study ... studi*ed*
> carry ... carri*ed*

Affirmative: I work*ed*.

Negative: We use the past tense of the verb *to do: did + not (didn't)*. The form is the same for all persons:

> I *did not (didn't)* work.
> She *did not (didn't)* work.

Interrogative: We put *did* before the subject:

> *Did* you work?
> *Did* he work?

Note: The Present Simple is used to talk about an action which happened at a specific time.

> We played football yesterday.

78

PRESENT AND PAST SIMPLE

AFFIRMATIVE

I You We They	work. worked.
He She It	works. worked.

NEGATIVE

I You We They	do not don't did not didn't	work.
He She It	does not doesn't did not didn't	work.

INTERROGATIVE

Do Did	I you we they	work?
Does Did	he she it	work?

1.6 QUESTION TAGS

We can make question tags with auxiliary verbs *to be* and *to have*.

> He isn't happy, *is he*?
> She has a headache, *hasn't she*?

We can also use the modal verbs.

> He lives here, *doesn't he*?
> She shouldn't go to the disco, *should she*?

We use a negative tag after an affirmative verb:

> He *speaks* English, *doesn't he*?

We use an affirmative tag after a negative verb:

> They *can't play* the piano, *can they*?

Note: We use question tags to check if someone agrees or disagrees with us.

1.7 THE PRESENT CONTINUOUS OR PRESENT PROGRESSIVE TENSE

Affirmative: We make the Present Continuous with the present of the verb to be as auxiliary, and we add *-ing* to the infinitive of the main verb.

> I am (I'm) going to the airport.

Negative: We put *not* between the auxiliary and the main verb.
> She is *not (isn't)* going to the airport.

Interrogative: We put the auxiliary before the subject:
> Are you going to the airport?

Note: We use the Present Continuous to talk about actions which are taking place at this moment.

We can also use the Present Continuous to talk about the future.

> *I'm going to* the airport *tomorrow*.

1.8 THE PAST CONTINUOUS OR PAST PROGRESSIVE TENSE

We make the Past Continuous in the same way as the Present Continuous, but using the past tense of the verb *to be: was* or *were*.

Affirmative: She *was eating* an ice-cream.

Negative: We *were not (weren't) playing* football.

Interrogative: *Were* they *watching* TV last night?

Note: We use the Past Continuous to talk about an action that took place in the past, and which was often completed by another action:

He *was sleeping* when the bell *rang.*

1.9 THE PRESENT PERFECT CONTINUOUS OR PRESENT PERFECT PROGRESSIVE TENSE

We make this tense with the verb *to be* in its Present Perfect forms, *has been* or *have been*, and we add the gerundive form of the verb.

Affirmative: *I have (I've) been watching* TV.

Negative: *She has not (hasn't) been playing* the piano.

Interrogative: *Have they been working?*

Note: We use this tense for an action which began in the past and which is still going on.

PRESENT, PAST AND PRESENT PERFECT CONTINUOUS

AFFIRMATIVE

I	am/'m was have been		
He She It	is/'s was has been	eating	an ice-cream.
You We They	are/'re were have been		

NEGATIVE

I	'm/am not was not haven't been	
He She It	is not/isn't was not/wasn't hasn't been	eating.
You We They	are not/aren't were not/weren't haven't been	

INTERROGATIVE

Am	I		
Was	I		
Have	I	been	
Is	he		
Was	she		eating?
Has	it	been	
Are	you		
Were	we		
Have	they	been	

1.10 THE FUTURE WITH 'GOING TO'

We often use *to be + going to +* the infinitive to talk about the future.

Affirmative: She *is going to learn* English.
They *'re going to play* tennis tomorrow.

Negative: He *isn't going to leave* until Sunday.
They *aren't going to see* the play.

Interrogative: *Aren't you going to come* on the trip tomorrow?
Isn't she going to sit the exam in June?

FUTURE WITH 'GOING TO'
AFFIRMATIVE/NEGATIVE

I	am/'m not		leave.
He She It	is not/n't	going to	fly.
You We They	are not/n't		play.

1.11 THE FUTURE WITH 'WILL'

We can also talk about the future by using *will* as an auxiliary to the main verb. All forms of the verb are identical.

Affirmative: *I will (I'll)* finish it tomorrow.

Negative: *She will not (won't)* go with you.

Interrogative: *Will they come today?*

FUTURE WITH 'WILL'

I He They	will (will not) 'll (won't)	finish.

Will	I/ he/she/it you/we/they	finish?

1.12 THE PRESENT PERFECT

We make the Present Perfect with *have* as the auxiliary and the past participle of the main verb: *play... have played.*

Affirmative: *I have* often *played* tennis.
                       He has moved it.

Negative: *I have not (haven't) done* my homework.
                       She has not (hasn't) finished the project.

Interrogative: *Have you moved* it?
                       Has she moved it?

Note: It is important to remember we use the Simple Past when an action has been completed, but the Present Perfect when an action continues into the present.

I lived in Paris in 1990.
I have lived here since 1990.

PRESENT PERFECT

AFFIRMATIVE/NEGATIVE   INTERROGATIVE

I You We They	have 've	n't not	seen moved	it.		Have	I you we they	seen moved	it?
He She It	has 's	n't not	torn found	them.		Has	he she it	torn found	them?

1.13 THE CONDITIONAL

A conditional statement has two parts:

a) the condition: *If John comes. ...*
b) the result: *... we'll go to the cinema.*

When we are talking about something in the future that is 'probable', we use *if* + present simple + *will, can, may:*

If you give me some money, *I'll* buy a present.
If she gets home early, *we can* go out for dinner.
If I have a holiday in December, *I may* go to Rome.

If we are talking about something that is only 'possible', not 'probable', we use *if* + past simple + *would, could, might.*

If I saved some money, *I would* come back next year.
If he studied harder, *he could* pass the exam.
If you got up early, *we might* catch the plane.

If	she you they	eats eat	them,	she you they	will be sick.
If	you	can't	come,	tell	me the problem.
If	I	were	you,	I	would do that.

1.14 THE IMPERATIVE

We make the imperative with the infinitive of the verb without *to*:

Affirmative: To look ... Look!
To be quiet ... Be quiet!

We make the negative by putting *don't* before the verb:

Negative: *Don't* look!
Don't be late!

Note: The singular and plural forms are the same.
We use the imperative form for orders, requests and suggestions.
We can use *please*, before or after the verb, to be less aggressive:

Please come in!
Stop here, please!

IMPERATIVE FORMS

> Take the M32. Don't take the M1.
> Try it! Don't be scared!

1.15 SHORT FORM ANSWERS

When a question can be answered with *yes* or *no*, we usually add a short form answer. We make this with the appropriate pronoun and the auxiliary verb.

Is she happy?
Yes, *she is.*
No, *she isn't.*

Do they live here?
Yes, *they do.*
No, *they don't.*

Note: When the short form answer is negative, we usually use the contracted form of *not: isn't, haven't, don't, can't.*
When the short form answer is affirmative, we never use the contracted form of the subject and verb.

SHORT FORM ANSWERS (YES/NO QUESTIONS)

Am Is Was Are Were	I he she you they	happy?	Yes,	I am. he is. she was. you are. they were.	No,	I'm not. he isn't. she wasn't. you aren't. they weren't.
Have Has	we got it got	a bag?	Yes,	we have. it has.	No,	we haven't. it hasn't.
Can Could Must Should Might	I we he they she	play the piano?	Yes,	I can. we could. he must. they should. she might.	No,	I can't. we couldn't. he mustn't. they shouldn't. she might not.
Do Does Did	they he she	live here?	Yes,	they do. he does. she did.	No,	they don't. he doesn't. she didn't.
Am Was Is Are Were	I he she we they	waiting for you?	Yes,	I am. he was. she is. we are. they were.	No,	I'm not. he wasn't. she isn't. we aren't. we weren't.
Am Is Are	I he you	going to stay?	Yes,	I am. he is. you are.	No,	I'm not. he isn't. you aren't.
Will	I/he/you	win?	Yes,	I/he will.	No,	he/you won't.
Has Have	she they	seen it?	Yes,	she has. they have.	No,	she hasn't. they haven't.

TAG QUESTIONS

Has Have	he you	been waiting?	Yes,	he has. I have.	No,	he hasn't. I haven't.
Is Was Are Were	this these	made in China?	Yes,	it is. it was. they are. they were.	No,	it isn't. it wasn't. they aren't. they weren't.
Is Was Are Were	there	a bank near here? any banks near here?	Yes,	there is. there was. there are. there were.	No,	there isn't. there wasn't. there aren't. there weren't.

I am He isn't She was You aren't They were	happy,	aren't I? is he? wasn't she? are you? weren't they?
We've got She hasn't got	a bag,	haven't we? has she?
I can't We could He must They shouldn't She might	play,	can I? couldn't we? mustn't he? should they? mightn't she?
They don't live He lives She didn't live	here,	do they? doesn't he? did she?
I am not He was She isn't We are They weren't	waiting,	am I? wasn't he? is she? aren't we? were they?
I'm not He is You aren't	going to eat,	am I? isn't he? are you?
You'll	win,	won't you?
She has They haven't	seen it,	hasn't she? have they?
He hasn't They've	been waiting,	has he? haven't they?

1.16 'There is' and 'There are'

We can use *there is* and *there are* as impersonal verbs:

Affirmative: *There is* a book on the chair.
There are some pictures on the wall.

Negative: *There isn't* any sugar.
There aren't any chocolates left.

Interrogative: *Is there* a banana in the fruit dish?
Are there any biscuits in the box?

We use *there was* and *there were* for the past:

Affirmative: *There was* some cheese on the table.
There were some CDs in my room.

Negative: *There wasn't* any wine left in the bottle.
There weren't any strawberries in the fridge.

Interrogative: *Was there* a new student in your class?
Were there any letters for me this morning?

We use *there will be* for the future:

Affirmative: *There will be* a concert tomorrow.

Negative: *There will not (won't) be* a trip on Saturday.

Interrogative: *Will there be* a train at midnight?
Will there be any buses on Sunday?

THERE IS/THERE ARE; THERE WAS/THERE WERE; THERE WILL BE

There	is/'s was isn't/wasn't	a picture some cheese (any)	on the table.
	are/'re were aren't/weren't	four bananas some biscuits (any)	
There	will be won't be	some showers rain/any rain any tornadoes	tomorrow morning.

Is Was	there	a picture any cheese	on the table?
Are Were		four bananas any biscuits	
Will there be	any	showers rain tornadoes	tomorrow morning?

1.17 THE PASSIVE VOICE

We make the passive with the verb *to be* + verb + *ed:*

Water *is warmed* by the sun.

We use the past tense of *to be* if we want to talk about the past:

Paper *was invented* 1900 years ago.

Note: The object of the active verb becomes the subject when the verb is in the passive:

Spain and Italy export *olive oil*.
Olive oil is exported by Spain and Italy.

If the subject of the passive verb is plural, then the verb is also plural:

Fiat cars are made in Turin.

THE PASSIVE VOICE

Cocoa Water This jacket	is	grown warmed made	in Ghana. by the sun. of leather.
Olives Fiat cars Bananas	are	grown made exported	in Greece. in Turin. to Europe.
Paper	can	be recycled.	

Paper The Palm House This plant	was	invented founded brought	1900 years ago. in 1759. to Kew in 1775.
Maize and beans These postcards Some children	were	grown sent bullied	by the Aztecs. from London. at school.
Chocolate	could	be drunk	in old Mexico.

2 THE ARTICLE

2.1 THE DEFINITE ARTICLE 'THE'

We use the definite article *the* for both singular and plural nouns.

The book   The books
The orange   The oranges

2.2 THE INDEFINITE ARTICLE 'A' OR 'AN'

We use the indefinite article only with singular nouns.
We use *a* before nouns which begin with a consonant: *a* book.
We use *an* before nouns which begin with a vowel: *an o*range.

Note: When the noun is plural, we use *some:*

Some books   Some oranges

3 *NOUN FORMS: POSSESSIVE*

When the noun is singular, we add *'s*:

> The boy*'s* teacher.
> The baby*'s* name.

When the noun is plural, and ends in *-s*, we just add an apostrophe (') after the noun:

> The boys' teacher.
> The babies' names.

4 *PRONOUNS AND ADJECTIVES*

4.1 DEMONSTRATIVES ('THIS', 'THAT', 'THESE', 'THOSE')

We use *this* when we speak about an object which is near the speaker.
The plural form is *these*.

> *This* is my book.
> *These* are my books.

We use *that* for objects which are not near the speaker:
The plural form is *those*.

> *That* book over there is Peter's.
> *Those* books over there are Peter's.
> *Those* are mine.

DEMONSTRATIVE PRONOUNS AND ADJECTIVES

	near	far	attributive	predicative
Singular	this (book)	that (book)	This is a good book.	It is heavy.
Plural	these (books)	those (books)	I've got some good books.	They are heavy.

4.2 PERSONAL PRONOUNS

Personal pronouns always accompany a verb, and can replace a noun subject:

> Andrea speaks English.
> *He* speaks English.

Personal pronouns can also replace nouns when these are the object of the verb:

> I can see Maria.
> I can see *her*.

> Can you help *me?*

4.3 POSSESSIVE ADJECTIVES

Possessive adjectives accompany the noun, and do not change their form:

> *My* brother is tall.
> *My* sister is tall, too.

> *My* books are quite interesting.

4.4 Possessive pronouns

We use these pronouns to avoid repeating words. They do not change their form:

> That is my horse.
> That is *mine*.

PRONOUNS AND ADJECTIVES

Personal Pronouns	Object Pronouns	Possessive Adjectives	Possessive Pronouns
I	me	my	mine
he	him	his	his
she	her	her	hers
it	it	its	
we	us	our	ours
you	you	your	yours
they	them	their	theirs

4.5 Indefinite pronouns 'some' and 'any'

We use *some* in affirmative sentences when we talk about plural or uncountable nouns:

> He wants *some chocolate*.
> She's going to buy *some ice-creams*.
> We changed *some money* yesterday.

We often use *any* when the sentences are negative or in questions:

> Have you got *any* biscuits?
> I don't want *any* chocolate.

SOME AND ANY

I've got		chocolate.
He wants	some	
Bring		biscuits.

Have you got		chocolate (?)
He doesn't want	any	
Don't bring		biscuits (?)

5 THE ADJECTIVE

5.1 Position

The adjective goes before the noun it qualifies:

> A *good book*.   A *nice person*.

When the adjective is used alone with the verb to be, it goes after the verb:

> It is *good*.   They are *nice*.

The form of the adjective does not change.

> A yellow train.
> Three yellow trains.
> This house is yellow.
> That pencil is yellow.

5.2 COMPARATIVES AND SUPERLATIVES

Adjectives with one or two syllables normally form the comparative by adding -er:

tall	tall*er*
quiet	quiet*er*

If they have more than two syllables, we normally put *more* before the adjective:

interesting	*more* interesting
expensive	*more* expensive

Adjectives with one or two syllables normally form the superlative by adding -est:

tall	tall*est*
quiet	quiet*est*

If they have more than two syllables, we normally put *most* before the adjective:

interesting	the *most* interesting
expensive	the *most* expensive

Note: There are some exceptions:

good	better	best
bad	worse	worst
far	farther/further	farthest/furthest

5.3 EQUALITY

We compare two equal things with *as* + adjective + *as* + noun:

> Sevilla is *as big as* Valencia.
> Madrid is *not as big as* New York.

	SHORT ADJECTIVES	OTHER ADJECTIVES
	Birmingham is a big city.	Birmingham is an expensive city.
COMPARATIVE	London is bigger than Birmingham.	London is more expensive than Birmingham.
SUPERLATIVE	Mexico city is the biggest of all.	Tokyo is the most expensive city of all.
EQUALITY	Tokyo is as big as London.	Paris is as expensive as London.
INEQUALITY	Los Angeles is not as big as New York.	Mexico City is not as expensive as London.
EXCEPTION	Molly is good at maths: Nina is better than Molly: Peter is the best in the class.	

6 *ADVERBS* The adjective describes the noun, and the adverb describes the verb:

> Andrew is *a careful driver.* (adj)
> Maria drives *carefully.* (adv)

6.1 ADVERBS OF MANNER

We make these by adding *-ly* to the adjective:

> nice   nice*ly*
>
> proper   proper*ly*

Note: *well* is the adverbial form of the adjective good.
fast and *hard* have the same form as adverbs or adjectives.

We normally put the adverb of manner at the end of the phrase:

> You must work *enthusiastically.*

ADVERBS OF MANNER (FORM AND POSITION)

adjective:	adverb:
careful	The mother looks after it carefully.
rough	He switches the machine on roughly.
clumsy	He pours the powder clumsily.
enthusiastic	You must work enthusiastically.

7 *PREPOSITIONS* ### FINAL POSITION OF PREPOSITIONS

In questions, any preposition will go at the end, not at the beginning:

> Where do you come *from?*
> What's the spoon *for?*
> Who are you travelling *with?*

The same thing happens in sentences which contain a relative pronoun or an adjectival clause:

> These are the people who Colin was talking *to.*
> That's the family I was staying *with.*

PREPOSITIONS (FINAL POSITIONS)

in questions:	What's your jacket made of? It's made of silk.
	Who are you travelling with? With a friend.
	How long are you staying for? For three weeks.
in adjectival clauses:	The boy Peter is coming with is called Rick.
	These are the boys who Colin was talking to.

INTERROGATIVE PRONOUNS (QUESTION WORDS)

What ...?   We use *what* to ask about actions or things:

                               What's your favourite sport?

Who ...?   We use *who* to ask about people:

                               Who wants an ice-cream?

Where ...?   We use *where* to ask about places:

                               Where do you come from?

Whose ...?   We use *whose* to ask about the possessor of an object:

                               Whose book is this?

How ...?   We use *how* to ask about someone's health, or to ask about an action:

                               How are you?
                               How do you make this soup?

How much ...? We use *how much* and *how many* to ask about quantity, distance and measurement:

                               How much does it cost?
                               How many records have you got?

QUESTION WORDS

What	is that?	It's	a Lamborghini.
Who			Miss Taylor.
Where			in Mexico.
Whose			Peter's (mine).

How	do you spell 'book'?	B-O-O-K.
	are you?	Fine, thanks.
	do you come to school?	By car.
	are they doing it?	By burning it.

What nationality is he?	He's Portuguese.
What time is it?	It's twelve o'clock.
What does it look like?	It's big and green.
What is it like?	It's brilliant!
What happened?	They disappeared.
Why can't you stay?	Because it's late.
Which is the newest ride?	The Balloon Ride.
When is the party?	It's on Sunday.

How much	is it? is there?	It's £3. There is a lot.
How many	are there?	There is only one. There are five.
How old	is she?	She's thirteen.
How often	do you go?	Twice a week.
How long	did you stay? is the plane?	Three weeks. 70.5 metres long.
How wide	is it?	60 metres wide.
How tall	are you?	About 1.50m.

ACKNOWLEDGEMENTS

The authors and publishers wish to acknowledge, with thanks, the following photographic sources:

Clive Barda pages 34 centre right, 34 centre left, 38 left; Barnaby's Picture Library pages 2 bottom left, 14 top right, 18 centre right, 22 left, 36 top right, 38 bottom right, 44; Jim Brownbill pages 2 centre left, 50 bottom left, 51 top right, centre, bottom right; Camera Press Ltd page 45 bottom right; J. Allan Cash Photolibrary pages 2 centre right, 7 top, 38 centre right; Chris Fairclough Colour Library pages 7 centre, 37; Sally & Richard Greenhill pages 2 centre right, bottom right, 4, 7 bottom, 14 bottom left, bottom right, 15 bottom left, bottom right, 17 top; Ronald Grant Film Archives page 45 top right; Guardian page 10; Hulton Picture Company pages 36 top left, bottom left, bottom right; King's Theatre, Portsmouth page 18 top left; Shelagh Latham page 50 centre left; Picturepoint Ltd pages 15 top left, 18 bottom left, 20, 34 centre right, 36 top centre, bottom centre, 38 top right, 45 centre left, 47 bottom left; Popperfoto pages 45 top left, centre left, centre bottom; Valerie Randall pages 2, 8 bottom right, 17 right, 18 centre left, bottom right, bottom left, 22 bottom, 46, 51 centre right; Redferns pages 34 top right, centre left, bottom centre, top right, bottom right, 45 bottom left, top centre, centre right, 47 top left; Alan Thomas pages 2, 17 left, 33, 50 top left, top right, centre right, bottom right, 51 bottom left; United Glass Ltd page 2 bottom left; Zefa Picture Library page 47 top right, bottom right.

Cover poster of 'Paint the Town by Tube' reproduced by courtesy of The London Transport Museum.

The authors and publishers also wish to thank the following who have kindly granted permission for the use of copyright material:

The Brighton Festival Society Ltd. for a page from the 1989 Brighton Festival Programme; Kevin Dunne for his article 'Rock Music and Education' in the *Melody Maker*, 12 September, 1992; Eastern Counties Newspapers Ltd. for extracts from the Entertainments page in 'Encore' May, 1992, and an article from *Eastern Daily Press*, May, 1992; Guardian News Service Ltd. for the feature 'Inside Out' from *The Guardian* 17 January, 1992; Harper-Collins Publishers Ltd. for the poem 'Interruption at the Opera House' by Brian Patten, from *The Irrelevant Song* published by Unwin Hyman Ltd; Oxford University Press for extracts from the *Oxford Advanced Learners' Dictionary* edited by A.S. Hornby; Pink Floyd Music Publishers for the lyrics of 'If' by Roger Waters Copyright © 1970; St. Martins Press Inc. for an extract from *Let's Go: Guide to Europe* Copyright © 1991 by Let's Go, Inc., a wholly owned subsidiary of Harvard Student Agencies Inc.

The publishers have made every effort to trace the copyright holders, but if they have inadvertently overlooked any they will be pleased to make the necessary arrangements at the first opportunity.

The publishers would like to thank the following institutions for their valuable assistance in the piloting of this material: Basil Paterson College, Edinburgh; Bell School of Languages, Norwich; EF International School of English, Hastings; Eurocentre, Cambridge; International House, London; International Language Academy, Torquay; Nord-Anglia International Limited, Cheadle; Pitman School of English, London; The Swan School of English, Oxford; The Swan School of English, Stratford.

The authors would like to give very special thanks to Antoinette and Branka, without whom this course cannot have been written. They would also like to thank the Bell School of Languages, Bowthorpe Hall, Norwich and The Richard Huish College, Taunton.

Artists: Lawrie Taylor and Clive Spong.
Design: Julian Holland Publishing Ltd, Somerset, UK.
Cover design: Indent, Reading, UK.

First published 1993
Reprinted 1993

Published by *Macmillan Publishers Limited*

ISBN 0 - 333 - 57842 - 2

Printed in Spain

A CIP catalogue record for this book is available from the
British Library.